THEMES
for early years

D0784042

MYSELF

LYNNE BURGESS

THEMES
for early years

Author Lynne Burgess
Editor Noel Pritchard
Assistant editor Joel Lane
Series designer Lynne Joesbury
Designer Anna Oliwa
Illustrations Chris Russell
Cover based on an illustration by Sue Coney
Action rhymes, Poems and Stories compiled by Jill Bennett
Songs compiled by Peter Morrell
Assemblies chapter by Barbara Zigliss

Designed using Aldus Pagemaker
Processed by Scholastic Limited, Leamington Spa
Printed in Great Britain by The Alden Press, Oxford

Published by Scholastic Ltd, Villiers House, Clarendon Avenue, Leamington Spa, Warwickshire CV32 5PR

© 1995 Scholastic Ltd   Text © 1995 Lynne Burgess
Reprinted 1995

The publishers gratefully acknowledge permission to reproduce the following copyright material:
© 1995 Clive Barnwell for 'Look right, look left', 'Shoe choose tune'; © 1995 Ann Bryant for 'The birthday song' and 'The tooth song'; © 1995 Debbie Campbell for 'It's hard to say you're sorry' and 'What's that face?'; © 1995 Pie Corbett for 'Animal sounds we can make', 'The new dungarees' and 'Quiet as mice'; © 1995 Gina Douthwaite for 'How do I feel?'; © 1995 John Foster for 'I like to hear', 'My shadow' and 'Walking round the zoo'; © 1991 Trevor Harvey for 'Bedtime in Summer' from *Poetry Corner* (1991, BBC), © 1993 Trevor Harvey for 'Sometimes I pretend' from *Pretending Poems*, compiled by John Foster (1993, Oxford University Press); © 1995 Ian R. Henderson-Begg for 'I'm alive shanty'; © 1995 Lynn Lickiss for 'Summer at the swimming pool' and 'Winter in Vermont'; © 1995 Rozalia Makinson for 'I can'; © 1995 Peter Morrell for 'That hat!'; © 1995 Judith Nicholls for 'Sniff and tickle', 'The I don't-want-to-go-to-bed dance!' and 'Who?'; Reed Consumer Books for 'The End' from *Now We Are Six* by A.A. Milne (1927, Methuen Children's Books); © 1995 Irene Yates for 'Everybody's different', 'Inside' and 'The story of Jairus' daughter'.
Every effort has been made to trace copyright holders and the publishers apologise for any inadvertent omissions.

British Library Cataloguing-in-Publication Data A catalogue record for this book is available from the British Library.

ISBN 0-590-53346-0

THEMES *for early years*

CONTENTS

INTRODUCTION 5

HOW TO USE THIS BOOK 6

TOPIC WEB 8-9

PREPARING FOR PRIMARY SCHOOL 10

ACTIVITIES

CHAPTER 1: WHAT DO I LOOK LIKE?

Heads, shoulders, knees and toes 11

My body book 12

Mirror activities 13

Self-portraits 14

Magic mirror 15

Tops and bottoms 16

Face puzzles 17

Baby match 18

CHAPTER 2: WHAT DO I WEAR?

Dressing up 19

What's in the bag? 20

Clapping clothes 21

Socks on the washing line 22

Shoe mimes 23

Hat game 24

Baby clothes 25

Birthday badge 26

CHAPTER 3: WHO SHARES MY HOME?

Family portraits 27

Puppet families 28

Family treasure hunt 29

Teddy bear family tree 30

Safely home 31

Dressing doll family 32

Birthdays 33

Keep baby safe 34

CHAPTER 4: WHAT CAN I DO?

'I can' poem 35

Sand timer challenges 36

Bean bags 37

My hands 38

Mark-making challenge 39

Our day 40

Working together 41

Body sounds 42

CHAPTER 5: HOW DO I FEEL?

Clown shapes 43

Good and bad news 44

The happiest day of my life 45

Face-paint fun 46

Tongue-twisters 47

Angry dance 48

Happy and sad music 49

Tunnel of fear 50

CHAPTER 6: HOW CAN I LOOK AFTER MYSELF?

Eat more fruit	51
Apricot milkshake	52
Wash your hands	53
Skeletons	54
Hoop game	55
Go to sleep	56
Road safety	57
Jairus' daughter	58

CHAPTER 7: DISPLAYS

Body parts	59
Shoe prints	60
Action words	61
Hair care	61

CHAPTER 8: ASSEMBLIES

Assembly on families	63
An assembly on things we can do	64
An assembly on birthdays	65

RESOURCES

SONGS

I'm alive shanty	67
The birthday song	68
That hat!	68
What's that face?	69
It's hard to say you're sorry	70
Shoe choose tune	71
I use my hands	72
The tooth song	73
Look right, look left	74
My shadow	74

ACTION RHYMES AND POEMS

Tommy Thumb	75
Here we go round the mulberry bush	75
I can	76
Inside	77
Sniff and tickle	77
The end	77
How do I feel? and I like to hear	78
Walking around the zoo	79
Quiet as mice	79
The I-don't-want-to-go-to-bed dance!	80
Animal sounds we can make	80
Who?	80
Sometimes I pretend	81
Bedtime in summer	81
My shadow	81

STORIES

The new dungarees	82
Summer at the swimming pool	83
Winter in Vermont	84
The story of Jairus' daughter	85
Everybody's different	86

ACTIVITY SHEETS

Jigsaw faces	88
Match the hats	89
Draw a route	90
Match the clothes	91
Bean bags	92
Clown faces	93
Draw a banana	94
Recipe pictures	95
RECOMMENDED MATERIALS	96

INTRODUCTION

'Myself' is one of the most popular topics for early years pupils. At this early age, children are often self-centred and eager to talk about themselves. It is also a useful means for adults to get to know children and for children to find out more about each other. 'Myself' provides an excellent initial topic for children first encountering a new educational setting, such as starting playgroup or nursery or beginning school.

Organising a topic can be a demanding and time-consuming task. This book aims to help early years educators by providing a comprehensive starting-point for a 'Myself' topic. It includes a detailed topic web to show the overall relationship to all areas of the curriculum, ideas for stimulus displays and suggestions for activities. Photocopiable sheets at the end of the book link with specific activities and offer a useful method of recording. Finding relevant resources for a topic can often prove difficult, so a selection of stories, rhymes and songs is included, together with a list of recommended materials.

USING THEMES

There are many ways of approaching a topic on 'Myself', and many sub-themes can be explored. This book covers such common themes as physical appearance (Chapters 1 and 2), family (Chapter 3), achievements (Chapter 4), emotions (Chapter 5) and health education (Chapter 6). Throughout these activities, children are encouraged to discover more about themselves and then to explore the wider world by looking at families, friends, their own educational setting (school, nursery or playgroup) and the local community.

Each child has a valuable contribution to make, because the themes allow them to work from firsthand experience and to build on previous knowledge. It also provides an opportunity for them to discuss their likes and dislikes and express their feelings and opinions. Through an exploration of the topic 'Myself', each child should increase their self-esteem and establish themselves as a valued member of the group.

CROSS-CURRICULAR LINKS

Many early years teachers choose to teach through cross-curricular topics because of the advantages offered by an integrated approach. Young children naturally make links across the curriculum and are not constrained by subject boundaries. When playing with a computer toy (such as a Roamer), a child will be eager to learn how to operate it and may spontaneously give the toy a name and characteristics, and invent a story around it. The child will not see these as separate subjects (Design and Technology and English), but will be learning holistically through play.

The topic offers the opportunity for children to develop a broad range of concepts, skills and attitudes in all curriculum areas within a relevant context. For example, communication skills will be extended as the children talk, draw, role-play and sing. Opportunities to explore numeracy will arise naturally as they play, cook, build and take part in games. Vital observation skills will be encouraged as children look at displays or investigate in detail an object, picture, tool or material. Personal and social skills will be developed as the children become more aware of themselves and their relationships with others. All these important areas, and many more, can be covered in a more meaningful way by adopting an integrated approach.

HOW TO USE THIS BOOK

The wealth of material in this book will help teachers to plan work for several weeks, if not a whole term. The length of time spent on the topic will depend greatly upon the response of the children. Very young children may only be able to sustain interest and enthusiasm in a topic for a short period. However, by dividing the topic into shorter sub-themes, the children's natural curiosity can easily be rekindled as each new aspect of the topic is introduced.

TEACHING STRATEGIES

The content of this book has been deliberately organised to allow flexibility of use. Some teachers will wish to use most of the material provided, while others may find it a useful dip-in resource to supplement their own ideas. In either case, it is important to adapt activities and choose resources to suit the needs of the individual children in your early years setting.

Similarly, there is no need to tackle the topic elements in exactly the order in which they appear in the book. You may decide to begin your topic by exploring the children's emotions, and so Chapter 5 ('How do I feel?') may become your best starting-point. The activities within each chapter can also be used in any order.

TOPIC WEB PLANNING

The topic web on pages 8-9 aids planning by showing clearly how each activity relates to the National Curriculum and Scottish 5–14 Guidelines. To ensure that the children receive a broad and balanced curriculum, the topic web has been designed with an even distribution of activities between subjects.

Although each activity has one main subject focus, most will also make important contributions to other subject areas. For example, an activity which has been identified as having a chiefly mathematical basis will often introduce new vocabulary, and so develop children's language skills.

ACTIVITY PAGES

Each chapter in this section focuses on a particular theme of the 'Myself' topic. A wide variety of activities are suggested, each one linked to a different subject in the curriculum. The main elements within each activity are listed below.

Objective

This identifies the main subject area and explains the purpose of the activity. Many of the activities, however, will involve skills from more than one curriculum area.

Group size

A suggestion is given for the appropriate group size, but individual circumstances may influence your choice of the number of children in the group. For example, having adult helpers may mean that more children can undertake the activity than is suggested.

What you need

This provides a list of materials and equipment needed before the activity can begin.

Preparation

Preparation work is necessary for some activities. This may involve making or setting out equipment. Alternatively, the children may need prior experience or knowledge which is essential to the success of the activity.

What to do

Step-by-step instructions are outlined on how to introduce the activity, and guidance is offered on what the children should do. Although precise instructions are given, a certain amount of flexibility is needed, and most of the activities can be adapted for different ability levels.

Discussion

This section outlines the main discussion points, though it is important to adopt a flexible approach and allow the children to lead the conversation into other, equally valid areas. Some activities may involve adult intervention throughout, while others may lend themselves to a summary discussion after the children have completed the task. Whenever possible, encourage the children to discuss ideas with a friend, an older child or an adult helper, as well as yourself.

Follow-up activities

This contains ideas for extending each activity, both within the same subject area and into associated areas. Be prepared to follow up any idea suggested by the children, even if it moves the topic on to a slightly different area you had not originally intended to cover. It is important to allow the children some self-directed tasks.

DISPLAYS

This chapter suggests ideas for setting up stimulus displays linked to the various themes in this book. For each display there is a list of the materials required, instructions on how to assemble them and points for discussion. Most of the displays are interactive, to encourage the children to become actively involved. Whenever possible, encourage the children to help gather and select resources and allow them to help assemble the display. Always allocate sufficient time for the children to examine the displays individually, and organise a group or class discussion time to talk about them.

ASSEMBLIES

This chapter provides ideas for planning assemblies related to the theme of 'Myself'. Each assembly has its own practical ideas on how the children can contribute, ways in which they can be encouraged to reflect on the theme they are covering and a suggested prayer and song.

RESOURCES SECTION

These chapters contain a useful selection of stories, poems, action rhymes and songs which link specifically with the 'Myself' topic. Much of the material is new and has been specially commissioned to complement the 'Myself' topic. All of these resources are photocopiable.

PHOTOCOPIABLE ACTIVITY SHEETS

This section includes eight pages of photocopiable activities. Each page links with a specific activity detailed earlier in the book. It is important to make sure that the children understand how to complete each sheet, and that any new vocabulary is explained. Allow time to discuss the completed sheet with each child in order to find out how much they have understood.

RECOMMENDED MATERIALS

This section gives details of story-books, information books, poetry, songs and works of art linked to the 'Myself' topic. Many of these resources can be borrowed from local libraries. Also remember to ask the children to bring in their own favourite stories, poems and songs which focus on this topic.

EXPRESSIVE ARTS

ART
Self-portraits	14
Family portraits	27
Mark-making challenge	39
Skeletons	54

MUSIC
Heads, shoulders, knees and toes	11
Clapping clothes	21
Body sounds	42
Happy and sad music	49
Go to sleep	56

PE/DRAMA
Shoe mimes	23
Bean bags	37
Angry dance	48
Hoop game	55

ENGLISH
My body book	12
Dressing up	19
Safely home	31
'I can' poem	35
Tongue-twisters	47

RE/RELIGIOUS AND MORAL EDUCATION
Magic mirror	15
Birthdays	33
Tunnel of fear	50
Jairus' daughter	58

Planning towards the National Curriculum and the Scottish 5–14 National Guidelines

MATHEMATICS

Socks on the washing line	22
Dressing doll family	32
Sand timer challenges	36
Clown shapes	43
Eat more fruit	51

ENVIRONMENTAL STUDIES

SCIENCE

Mirror activities	13
What's in the bag?	20
Keep baby safe	34
My hands	38
Apricot milkshake	52
Wash your hands	53

TECHNOLOGY

Face puzzles	17
Birthday badge	26
Puppet families	28
Working together	41
Face-paint fun	46

HISTORY/PEOPLE IN THE PAST

Baby match	18
Baby clothes	25
Teddy bear family tree	30
Our day	40
The happiest day of my life	45

GEOGRAPHY/PEOPLE AND PLACE

Tops and bottoms	16
Hat game	24
Family treasure hunt	29
Good and bad news	44
Road safety	57

PREPARING FOR PRIMARY SCHOOL

The children in any early years setting are individuals, and many will be at very different stages of development. Whatever level they have reached, it is important to help prepare a sound foundation from which children can go on to study the subjects of the National Curriculum. This can easily be achieved through many everyday play activities.

The National Curriculum was established to standardise the subjects, and subject content, taught at all levels of a child's education. It is intended that any child will be able to go to school anywhere in the country and find the same areas of the curriculum being covered for the same amount of time every week. These subjects are: English, Mathematics, Science, History, Geography, Design and Technology, Information Technology, RE, Art, Music and PE.

Most of the activities suggested in this topic are based on common play activities such as dressing up, drawing, using construction toys or making puppets. However, each activity also has a specific objective: to develop important skills in preparation for the first stage of the National Curriculum.

TOWARDS LEVEL ONE

National Curriculum learning requirements do not apply until children reach the age of five. The National Curriculum programmes of study were therefore written to suit the abilities of children who have reached their fifth birthday and have spent anything from a term to a year (depending on the part of the country in which they live) in a Reception class. The National Curriculum provides an overall programme of study for each subject and asks teachers to assess the level of attainment of each child in the country when they reach Year Two. This assessment is carried out partly through nationwide testing; but for the most part, it is left to the teacher's professional judgement to allocate an overall level to each child.

By the time children begin Level 1, they will need to have developed vital learning skills. These include communication, observation, social skills and physical skills. The activities suggested in this book allow for these vital skills to be developed through firsthand experience.

The Topic Web on pages 8–9 also shows how the learning objective of each activity relates to the subject areas of the National Curriculum.

THE SCOTTISH NATIONAL GUIDELINES 5–14

In Scotland, there are National Guidelines for schools on what should be taught to children between the ages of five and fourteen.

These National Guidelines are divided into six main curriculum areas: English Language, Mathematics, Environmental Studies, Expressive Arts, Religious and Moral Education, and finally Personal and Social Development.

Within these main areas, further subjects are found – for example, 'Expressive Arts' includes art and design, drama, music and PE. Strands are also identified within each subject – for example, Mathematics includes Problem-solving and enquiry and Shape, position and movement.

Most nurseries will find that the experiences they are offering children will provide a good foundation for this curriculum. The activities in this book have been specially written to prepare for many aspects of it, and they will also fit well into the pre-five curriculum guidelines issued by local authorities throughout Scotland.

We have organised the activities into separate areas of the curriculum on the Topic Web on pages 8–9 to help you with your planning. The children's personal and social development is an ongoing theme that is incorporated throughout the activities in this book.

CHAPTER 1
WHAT DO I LOOK LIKE?

The activities in this chapter concentrate on physical appearance and encourage young children to name and describe their own body parts. When you lead children to compare themselves with others, start with similarities before exploring differences. Be sensitive to the feelings of individuals, and promote respect for diversity of appearance.

HEADS, SHOULDERS, KNEES AND TOES

Objective

Music – To learn a song and sing as part of a group. The song also involves the use of silence and miming actions.

Group size

Any size.

What you need

A copy of the song 'Heads, shoulders, knees and toes' (in *Okki-Tokki-Unga*, A & C Black).

What to do

Teach the song to the children, asking them to touch each part of their body as it is named. When they are familiar with the song, ask them to point to the body parts on a partner as they sing. Then introduce the idea of substituting silence for each word in turn, and mime touching each body part. For example, sing the song, missing out the word 'heads' each time. Then repeat the song, missing out the next word (body part) each time until the whole song is being mimed.

Discussion

Encourage the children to sing together and point to the body parts at the same time. Talk about the different types of movement each body part can make, and challenge the children to demonstrate various ways of moving their heads or shoulders. Which parts move least or most? Emphasise the need for the children to sing the missing words silently to themselves in order to follow the song.

Follow-up activities

◇ Link the song with the display idea on page 59. As you sing the song, ask a child to point to the body parts on the picture.
◇ Encourage the children to make up their own version of the song, using other body parts. For example, 'Neck, elbows, heels and wrists'.

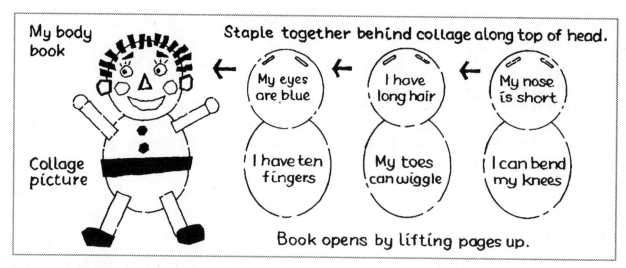

My body book · Collage picture · Staple together behind collage along top of head. · My eyes are blue · I have long hair · My nose is short · I have ten fingers · My toes can wiggle · I can bend my knees · Book opens by lifting pages up.

MY BODY BOOK

Objective

English — To encourage children to write a description of themselves which will accompany a collage picture.

Group size

Up to six children.

What you need

Sugar paper, gummed paper, tissue paper, wool, PVA adhesive, glue sticks, scissors, felt-tipped pens, a stapler.

Preparation

Cut the sugar paper into small circles (in a range of flesh tones) for heads and larger ovals (in any colour) for bodies. Cut sugar paper strips (in a variety of widths and colours) for arms and legs.

What to do

Allow the children to choose a flesh-toned circle for their head. Talk about the features on their head and encourage them to cut or tear collage shapes for hair, ears, eyes, nose, mouth and so on. Stick them on to the circle shape.

Allow the children to choose a large oval shape for their body and talk about the position of their arms, hands, legs and feet. Ask them to use the collage materials to represent these features. Very young children may find it easier to cut or tear the prepared strips of sugar paper to the required length, while more able children may be capable of cutting their own. Do the children want to add small items of clothing such as belts or buttons? Stick the head on to the body and allow to dry.

Invite the children to choose another head and body from the pieces of sugar paper. Ask them to write descriptions of their paper body on these shapes, using the felt-tipped pens. Act as scribe if necessary. Stick the head to the body and allow to dry. Repeat this process on further pieces of paper, until the children have finished writing. Help each child to assemble a book and staple it together along the top (as shown above).

Discussion

As the children make the collage body pictures, encourage them to describe themselves in detail. What colour are their eyes? Is their hair short or long, straight or curly? How many fingers do they have? Such questions will help to inspire their descriptive writing.

Encourage the children to experiment with the collage materials, creating different textures by bending, twisting, folding or scrunching them.

Follow-up activities

✧ Display the children's body books in the reading corner. Encourage the children to read them individually, in groups or with an adult. Once they are familiar with the books, suggest they take turns to choose one and describe its contents to the rest of the group.
✧ Add simple information books about the body to the display.

MIRROR ACTIVITIES

Objective

Science — To encourage careful observations of body parts and demonstrate the basic properties of mirrors.

Group size

Six children.

What you need

Three small glass mirrors (shaving or make-up mirrors), six small pieces of mirror card (available from educational suppliers), two large pieces of mirror card, adhesive tape.

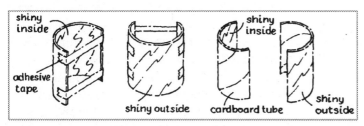

Preparation

Make concave and convex mirrors by bending the large pieces of mirror card. Use adhesive tape to fix them in position, or stick them on to the inside and outside of half a cardboard tube as shown above.

What to do

Ask the children to find a partner. Give each pair a small glass mirror. Suggest that they take turns to look into the mirror and describe their own reflection to their partner. Compare what they see when they are standing close to the mirror and when they are standing far away. Explain that glass mirrors are dangerous to play with, and introduce the mirror card. Compare the properties of the mirror card with those of the glass mirrors.

Give each child a small piece of mirror card. Then ask them to look into the mirror and describe what is behind them. Encourage them to move to different positions in the room and compare what they can see. Ask them to work in pairs: one child looks into her mirror, while the other walks in a circle around the first child until she can be seen in the mirror.

Suggest the children take turns to look into the concave and convex mirrors. Talk about what happens to their reflection with each one.

Discussion

Name body parts as the children talk about their reflections. How much of their body can they see in the mirror? Does this change if they stand near or far away from the mirror? Which parts of their body move if they wave or wink at their reflection?

Compare the materials used to make the glass mirrors and the mirror card. How well do they reflect? Which one is flexible? Discuss how mirrors are used for various purposes, for example, on cars or at the dentist. Name other items in which the children have seen their reflections, such as spoons, kettles, shiny paint on cars, Christmas baubles and so on. Did any of these distort the shape of their body parts?

Follow-up activities

◇ Give each child a piece of mirror card and ask the children to work in pairs. Challenge them to arrange the two pieces of card together in different positions, taking turns to hold the cards or look into the mirror. Encourage them to describe what happens to their reflection.

◇ Sing the 'I'm alive shanty' from the Resources section on page 67.

SELF-PORTRAITS

Objective

Art – To draw self-portraits from observation.

Group size

Up to six children.

What you need

A piece of mirror card for each child, two or three framed portrait photographs, grey sugar paper, charcoal, chalks or pastels, scissors, PVA adhesive, glue sticks, fixative spray.

What to do

Give each child a mirror card and talk to them about their reflections. Encourage them to concentrate on their faces, naming and describing the various parts. Ask them to use the charcoal and chalks to draw large pictures of their own faces on pieces of grey sugar paper. Show them how they can blend colours by smudging with their fingers and create new colours by overlapping. Invite them to look into the mirror for details to include in their portraits.

Show the children the portrait photographs and talk about how they are framed. Cut some grey sugar paper into narrow strips to be used to make a frame. Suggest that they use the chalks to colour the strips, smudging the colours to blend them; then help them to measure and cut their strips to the right length to form a frame around their portrait. Stick the frame on and spray the portrait with fixative (following the manufacturer's instructions).

Display the finished portraits and discuss the results with the children.

Discussion

Focus the children's attention on their faces by talking about the colour of their eyes, the shape of their noses and the length and texture of their hair. How many eyebrows, ears, nostrils and chins do they each have? Talk about any distinctive features such as freckles, hairbands or earrings. What sort of expressions will they draw on their faces?

Compare a photograph with a drawing. Describe how each one is made and find similarities and differences between them. Discuss whether the children prefer pictures and photographs with or without a frame.

Follow-up activity

Find two different self-portraits, painted by famous artists in the past. Explain that portraits were often painted in the past because photographs were not available. Compare and contrast the two portraits. Identify the various body parts and discuss the appearance of each one (male, female, young, old, physical attributes, clothing, hairstyle). Talk about the feelings conveyed in each portrait. What else can we tell about the people in the paintings? Describe the frames of the pictures (if visible).

MAGIC MIRROR

Objective

RE – To discuss what the children like and dislike about their appearance.

Group size

Up to six children.

What you need

A large piece of mirror card, card, small pieces of coloured foil and Cellophane (sweet wrappers), PVA adhesive, adhesive tape, white paper, black felt-tipped pens, white drawing paper, pencils, wax crayons, a display board, a stapler.

Preparation

Make a 'magic mirror' with the mirror card. Stick small pieces of coloured foil and Cellophane on to strips of card. When these are dry, use adhesive tape to stick them to the mirror card to make a frame.

Draw speech bubble shapes on to the white paper, then cut them out. (See illustration.)

What to do

Ask the children what they like most about their own appearance. Then give an example of something that you dislike about your own appearance and describe how you would like to change it. Show the children the 'magic mirror' and explain that they are all going to pretend the magic mirror will grant each of them one wish that will change one aspect of their own appearance. Suggest that they take turns to look into the magic mirror and say their wish out loud. For example, 'Magic mirror on the wall, will you make my hair grow long and curly?' As the children talk, write each wish on one of the speech bubbles.

Ask the children to draw and colour in a picture of themselves. Staple the magic mirror to a display board, then surround it with the children's drawings of themselves and their speech bubble wishes.

Discussion

Help the children to realise that most people like and dislike things about their own appearance. Point out any advantages of physical attributes that the children dislike. For example, being tall or having short hair can have positive aspects. Encourage the children to be sensitive to each other's feelings during discussion.

Follow-up activities

✧ Read stories which deal with differences in appearances – *Tall Inside* by Jean Richardson and Alice Englander (Picture Puffin), *The Ugly Duckling* by Hans Christian Andersen (Ladybird/others), *Elmer* by David McKee (Andersen Press).
✧ Read the story 'Everybody's different' from the Resources section on page 86.

child's drawing

speech bubble dictated by child

Card frame decorated with coloured foil and Cellophane (sweet wrappers)

TOPS AND BOTTOMS

Objective

Geography – To extend awareness of the world by examining the diversity of human appearance.

Group size

Up to six children.

What you need

Eight pictures of people of different nationalities (good sources are magazines, newspaper supplements, calendars from shops such as Oxfam), card, adhesive plastic film, scissors, adhesive, a globe.

Preparation

Mount the pictures on to separate pieces of card and cover with adhesive plastic film. Cut each picture into two pieces horizontally.

What to do

Mix up the pieces of the pictures and ask the children to work together to match the top halves to the bottom halves. When they have finished, talk about the similarities and differences between the people. Explain that they live in different countries, and find out if the children can name the countries where these people were born. Use the globe to show the birthplace of each child and then to find the countries of origin of the people in the pictures.

Discussion

Encourage the children to identify the common physical characteristics of all the people (hands, eyes, arms, legs). Then look for differences in age, gender, physical appearance, expression, clothing and any background details. What can the children tell about each person? Is it possible to determine whether they live in a hot or a cold country?

Some young children will have no concept of the wider world, while others will display a surprising level of knowledge. Look at a globe (world map) with them. Can they distinguish the sea areas from the land? What are the usual differences?

Follow-up activities

✧ Read the stories 'Summer at the swimming pool' and 'Winter in Vermont' in the Resources section on pages 83 and 84.

✧ Choose one aspect of physical appearance (such as height, eye colour or hair colour) for comparison. Record the similarities and differences between the children in picture form (see examples above).

FACE PUZZLES

Objective

Technology – To make a simple puzzle.

Group size

Six children.

What you need

Two simple puzzle pictures of faces (one made from wood and one from card), white drawing paper (in two sizes), pencils, wax crayons, coloured card, PVA adhesive, glue sticks, adhesive plastic film, scissors.

What to do

Divide the children into two groups of three and give each group a puzzle to do. When they have finished, ask the children to compare the pictures on the puzzles and the materials used to make them. Explain that they are going to make their own card puzzle of a face.

Allow the children to choose the size of their drawing paper and ask them to draw a large face on it. Emphasise the need to colour it in carefully with the wax crayons. Invite the children to choose the colour of their backing card and stick their picture on to it. Help them to cover it with adhesive plastic film. Suggest that they cut their puzzle into a few large pieces (four to six) rather than lots of little pieces. Children who find scissors too difficult can draw lines on the back of the puzzle for an adult to cut along.

Invite the children to piece their own puzzle back together and then swap puzzles with other members of the group. Comments about mixing up the pieces of different puzzles can lead into the Follow-up activities (see text below).

Discussion

Talk about the kind of face the children are drawing. Will it be male or female, old or young? Remind them to look at each other's faces for ideas on colour of eyes, length of hair, shape of nose and so on. Discuss whether they will include any unusual features such as glasses, hairbands or beards.

When the children have tried out the puzzles, talk about how well they work. Which is the easiest one to do? Which is most difficult and why? What are the difficult aspects of piecing together the puzzles? How could these be overcome next time?

Follow-up activities

✧ Suggest that the children decorate envelopes to store their puzzle pieces in. Write each child's name on the front, and allow them to choose their own materials and type of decoration.
✧ Give the children the photocopiable sheet on page 88 and ask them to draw lines to match the missing puzzle pieces to the correct puzzles. Ask them to name the parts of the human face shown on each missing piece.

BABY MATCH

* *

Objective

History – To identify differences between photographs of the children as babies and at their present age.

Group size

Up to six children.

What you need

Two photographs of each child (one as baby and one at present), 12 small plastic wallets, 18 small pieces of card, felt-tipped pens, two large pieces of card, adhesive tape, two small pictures – a buggy and a bike (these can be found in catalogues).

Preparation

Put each photograph into its own small plastic wallet. Write each child's name on a small piece of card and slide it into the wallet behind the matching photograph (name side facing outward). Now make name cards by writing each child's name again on to a separate small piece of card.

Make card pockets to store the photographs in. Cut two small pieces of card and fix them to a large piece of card using adhesive tape. Make sure they are large enough to hold the photographs. Stick a picture of a buggy on to the first pocket and label it 'babies', then stick the bike picture on to the other pocket and label it 'children'. Put the photographs into the correct pockets.

What to do

Show the children the card pocket containing the child photographs. Invite each child to choose a photograph and look at it carefully. Ask each child to describe their photograph to the others and see if the others can name the child shown. Show them the name on the reverse side. Were they right? Repeat with the baby photographs.

Mix the cards up, then ask the children to take turns to choose one and place it in the correct pocket. This will help to establish whether the children can tell the difference between the photographs of babies and the photographs of children.

Show the children the name cards and ask them to find their own names. Remove the photographs from the pockets and mix them up. Ask the children to match both of the photographs of themselves to their name cards. Extend the activity by repeating the process, but asking each child to match the photographs and name card for someone else in the group. The children can find out if they have the correct photographs by checking the names on the reverse sides.

Discussion

As the children look at the photographs, encourage them to talk about how they have changed. What is different about their physical appearance? Are there any differences in clothing? Can they identify any changes in their abilities, such as the change from crawling to walking? Look to see whether it is easier to match some baby to child photographs because of obvious similarities, such as the same red hair or expression.

Compare all the photographs of the babies and look for similarities and differences. Is it possible to tell which is the youngest or oldest baby? Then compare all the photographs of the children and look for similarities and differences. Have they all grown to the same size?

Follow-up activities

✧ Suggest that the children write or dictate a few sentences about their own photographs. Mount each child's photographs and writing together and display them.

✧ Read the poem 'The end' in the Resources section on page 77.

CHAPTER 2
WHAT DO I WEAR?

Clothes are an important part of our self-image, and young children quickly develop strong preferences. This chapter focuses on naming and describing a wide range of clothing, and discusses why and when these clothes would normally be worn. Many of the activities encourage children to observe and describe the properties of materials.

DRESSING UP

Objective

English – To name and describe articles of clothing. To record the results of the dressing-up activity in writing.

Group size

Up to six children.

What you need

A selection of dressing-up clothes, large boxes, labels, felt-tipped pens, adhesive tape, a large safe mirror, a Polaroid camera, writing paper, pencils, glue sticks, card for mounting, a small plastic box.

Preparation

Invite the children to help sort the dressing-up clothes into separate boxes according to the type of clothing, such as hats, belts, bags, shirts and so on. Be sure to include items of clothing which will appeal both to boys and to girls. Attach a simple word and picture label to each box. Then cut the card for mounting into rectangles, allowing enough space for a photograph and a brief written description. These cards should be of a suitable size to stand upright in the plastic box. Label the plastic box appropriately, for example: 'Abracadabra, look how I have changed!'

What to do

Invite each child to name and describe the clothes they are wearing. Challenge them to change their appearance using the dressing-up clothes. When they are satisfied with their new clothes, take a photograph (using a Polaroid camera) of each child saying 'Abracadabra'. Stick the photograph on to the mounting card and ask each child to dictate or write a brief description of what they are wearing. Also encourage them to describe the type of character they have become. Store the 'Abracadabra' cards upright in the plastic box. Allow the children time to play together in their new clothes and then return the clothes to the correct box.

Discussion

When talking to the children about their own clothes, encourage them to describe the colours, textures and decoration as well as identifying common types of materials (wool, plastic, metal, leather). Ask them about their likes and dislikes. What are their favourite clothes?

As the children dress up, encourage them to help each other with difficult clothing. In what order do they put clothes on? Talk about the different methods of fastening various garments, and discuss how easy these are to use.

Invite the children to use the mirror to assess their changing appearance and choose alternative items if they wish. Talk about the reasons for their choices. Are they choosing clothes which are all the same colour? What sort of character is emerging as they dress up?

When photographing the children, encourage them to adopt a pose and expression to match their clothing. When recording the description of their new outfit, ask for details. What type of hat are they wearing? What colour cardigan? What material is the belt made of? Have they changed (for instance) into an old lady carrying a heavy bag of shopping, or a character from a story?

Follow-up activity

The 'Abracadabra' cards can also be used as accessories to storytelling and for sorting activities.

WHAT'S IN THE BAG?

Objective

Science — To identify items of clothing by touch and describe their properties.

Group size

Any size.

What you need

A drawstring bag, five or six items of clothing (hat, belt, shoe, jumper, swimsuit, shorts).

Preparation

Place the items of clothing inside the drawstring bag without the children seeing them.

What to do

Tell the children you have several different sorts of clothing inside the bag. Ask each child in turn to put one hand into the bag, choose an article to describe and identify it by touch alone. Then invite the child to take the article out of the bag to see if they have guessed correctly.

Change the items once the children are familiar with them. Increase the level of difficulty by including two items which are similar. For example, use two items of footwear (a trainer and a boot) or two hats (a rain hat and a bobble hat) and see if the children can distinguish between the two.

Discussion

Encourage each child to describe the item they are touching in detail, and use questions to extend their descriptive abilities. Is it hard or soft? Does it stretch or bend? What shape can you feel? What kind of material is it made out of? Can you feel any fastenings? Is it rough or smooth, thick or thin?

Talk about when and why each garment would be worn. Is it suitable for hot or cold weather? Would it be worn every day, or on a special occasion?

Follow-up activities

✧ Ask each child to choose an item of clothing from the bag, draw a picture of it and write or dictate a detailed description of it on a separate piece of paper. Mount these as 'lift the flap' activities on to a large piece of sugar paper shaped like a drawstring bag, with a 'string' made from real string or wool. The children can read a description, guess what item is being described and then lift the flap to see if they were correct.

✧ Read the story 'The New Dungarees' in the Resources section on page 82.

CLAPPING CLOTHES

Objective

Music – To clap simple rhythms to accompany words.

Group size

Any size.

What you need

Five or six articles of clothing (skirt, belt, trainers, sari, petticoat, cardigan).

What to do

Ask the children to sit in a circle. Place the articles of clothing in the middle. Select a child to choose one item of clothing and ask her to name it. Show the children how to clap the name of the item (one clap per syllable) and ask them to join in with you. Repeat this for each item of clothing. Once the children are used to this, clap the rhythm for the name of each garment as it is held up and ask the

children to name it. Invite them to say and clap it again without you. Clap simple rhythms (one, two or three claps) and ask the children to suggest any item of clothing to fit that rhythm.

If very young children find clapping a difficult co-ordination task, suggest they slap their knees instead.

Discussion

As the name of each garment is clapped, ask the children to count the number of claps. Which clothes have most or fewest claps? Which ones have the same number of claps? How many items of clothing can the children suggest for two claps? Can they suggest something for four claps?

Follow-up activity

Extend this activity into a circle clapping game. Choose one child to start the game and ask her to name and clap the rhythm for any item of clothing. The rest of the group repeat the name and the clapping. The next child must choose a different item of clothing and repeat the activity. Continue the game until each child has had a turn.

SOCKS ON THE WASHING LINE

Objective

Mathematics — To compare and order socks according to length.

Group size

Two or three children.

What you need

A large piece of card, felt-tipped pens, six to eight socks of different lengths, a sand timer.

Preparation

Draw a straight washing line between two large posts on the card. This needs to be large enough to 'hang' the socks on.

What to do

Allow the children to handle the socks and talk about the similarities and differences between them. Then focus their attention on the length of each sock. Give them the picture of the washing line and explain that all the socks have been blown off the line. Challenge them to put the socks back on to the line in order, from the shortest to the longest. Use the sand timer to limit the time for this task.

When the children can complete the activity easily, increase the number of socks or reduce the time allowed.

Discussion

Encourage the children to describe in detail the colour, texture and decoration of the socks. Can they identify whether the sock would be worn by a child or an adult? Does the sock have a particular function, such as a football sock or a 'Christmas stocking'?

Make sure the children understand that a true comparison of size can only be made if the socks have a common starting level. Demonstrate this with two socks on the picture of the washing line, emphasising the need for the top of each sock to touch the straight line.

Discuss whether the children were able to complete the activity easily within the time allowed. What difficulties arose, and how could these be overcome in future?

Follow-up activity

The children can paint giant socks with interesting patterns on them. Ask more mature children to devise repeating patterns on the socks. Cut the socks out and mount them in order of length on a washing line picture. Make the socks easily detachable, so they can be mixed up for the children to reorder correctly.

SHOE MIMES

❖❖❖❖❖❖❖❖❖❖❖❖❖❖❖❖❖❖❖❖❖❖❖❖❖❖❖

Objective

PE – To use movement in making different responses to a variety of shoes.

Group size

Any size.

What you need

A collection of footwear which will provoke a range of movements (Wellington boots, football boots, high-heeled shoes, ballet shoes, tap shoes), a tambourine and beater, an area large enough for movement activities.

What to do

As a warm-up activity, ask the children to pretend to shake their shoes off, both on the spot and while on the move.

Display the collection of shoes at the front of the movement area. Ask the children to name each type of shoe, and explain that they are going to pretend to put each pair on and move as they would when wearing them. Invite a child to choose a pair for the first mime. Use the tambourine to accompany the movement and to signal the start and finish. A tambourine is a versatile choice of instrument: it can be banged loudly, brushed gently or shaken softly, or the wooden edge can be tapped with the sharp end of the beater. Try to choose a sound which will match each type of shoe. More experienced children could be asked to suggest ways of playing the tambourine to accompany each mime.

Discussion

As each pair of shoes is chosen, allow the children some time to explore their own movement ideas freely. Then broaden the range of movements by introducing more structured suggestions. For example:

Wellington boots – stamping in mud, jumping in puddles, dragging through water, kicking piles of dead leaves.

Football boots – running or jogging in different directions at different speeds, kicking, dribbling, jumping to head a ball.

High heels – walking on tiptoes, walking daintily around mud or puddles, falling over.

Ballet shoes – leaping and gliding, twisting and turning, moving high and low with pointed toes.

Tap shoes – experimenting to make as many different sounds as possible, both loud and soft, with different parts of their feet.

Follow-up activities

❖ Put all the pairs of shoes into a box and challenge the children to work together to find the matching pairs as quickly as possible. Use a sand timer to limit the time allowed.

❖ Sing the song 'Shoe choose tune' from the Resources section on page 71.

HAT GAME

* *

Objective

Geography – To match hats to people with different occupations. This will help children to recognise that people can perform a variety of jobs and that some jobs can be associated with particular clothing.

Group size

Up to six children.

What you need

Six hats associated with jobs (for example, nurse, fire-fighter, police officer, lollipop person, cook, postal worker), a picture of someone dressed in the uniform associated with each hat (remember to find a balance of male and female representatives), six small boxes (large enough for each hat to sit on), six pieces of sugar paper (each a different colour), PVA adhesive, Blu-Tack.

Preparation

Make the six boxes more attractive by covering them with sugar paper (one colour for each box). Use the Blu-Tack to stick a picture of a different worker on one side of each box. Then cut a circle from each sheet of sugar paper (just large enough to cover the head on each picture).

What to do

Display the six boxes on a small table with the pictures facing the front. Gather the children round the table so that they can see the boxes clearly. Identify the occupation of the person in each picture, and talk about their clothing and especially their hats. Show the children the hats and discuss each one. Invite the children to match the hats to the pictures by placing the correct hat on top of each box. Once the children can do this easily, use the small circle of sugar paper to conceal the head of each person on the pictures temporarily. Repeat the hat matching task.

Discussion

Talk about the function of the clothing worn by the people in the pictures. Why does a fire-fighter need leggings? How does a fluorescent tabard or armband help a lollipop person? Look at each hat and describe its size, colour, shape and weight. Allow the children to try on the different hats. Discuss how the design and materials used help the person perform their job. Why does a cook need a hat? Why does a policeman's helmet need to be hard? Ask the children to say which hat they would most like to wear and why. What other types of headgear do they wear?

Follow-up activities

✧ Put the hats into the dressing-up box to encourage role-play. Ask individuals to choose a hat, wear it and mime an appropriate action. Can the other children name the occupation and identify what the person is doing?
✧ Extend this activity by giving the children the photocopiable sheet on page 89. Talk about the people and hats shown on the sheet, and ask the children to draw a line to match the correct hat to each person.
✧ Sing the song 'That hat!' from the Resources section on page 68.

BABY CLOTHES

∗ ∗

Objective

History – To identify the differences between clothing worn as a baby and as a child.

Group size

Up to six children.

What you need

A selection of clothing suitable for a baby (nappy, vest, Babygro, cardigan, hat), clothing suitable for a child (pants, vest, shorts, T-shirt, hat), a small suitcase, a baby doll, two labels, felt-tipped pens, two set rings.

Preparation

Put the items of clothing into the small suitcase. Make two labels: 'Clothes for a baby' and 'Clothes for us'.

What to do

Show the children the baby doll, and explain that some of the clothes in the suitcase are for the doll and some are for a child. Place the two set rings on the floor with a label in each, then place the doll near the appropriate label to help the children distinguish which ring is which. Challenge the children to take the clothing out of the suitcase and place it in the correct ring.

Discussion

Once the children have sorted the clothes, talk about each item in turn. Name the article and discuss which part of the body it fits. Discuss the size, shape, colour, texture and decoration. What fastenings are there? Have the clothes been correctly allocated to their sets?

Talk about the differences between the clothes for a baby and those for a child. As well as discussing obvious differences in size, can the children identify changes in development? For example, compare the nappy with the pants.

Follow-up activities

✧ Invite the children to bring in items for a display to show what they wore as a baby and what they wear now. As well as clothing, the children could bring photographs. Encourage them to gain information from their parents.

✧ Record this information by giving each child a piece of paper with two large set rings drawn on it. Label one ring 'When I was a baby, I wore . . .' and the other 'Now I am four, I wear . . .' Ask the children to draw clothes (or stick pictures from clothing catalogues) inside the correct rings.

Clothes for a baby

Clothes for us

BIRTHDAY BADGE

Objective

Technology – To make a badge to celebrate each child's age.

Group size

Up to six children.

What you need

A collection of badges showing different ages, card in different colours, pencils, scissors, a choice of colouring media (such as wax crayons, coloured pencils and felt-tipped pens), six pieces of Velcro, adhesive tape.

What to do

Show the children the collection of badges and talk about their size, shape, colour, decoration and construction. Identify the number on each badge and establish the age of each child. Tell the children they are going to make their own badges and invite them to discuss the possible designs. Young children could describe their thoughts verbally, while older children could draw their ideas.

Allow each child to choose a piece of coloured card and ask them to draw the overall shape of their badge, cut out the shape and draw on the number of their age (provide assistance when necessary). Invite each child to decorate their badge with the media of their choice. When the badges are finished, help each child to stick or sew a piece of Velcro on to the back.

Discussion

As the children handle and discuss the collection of badges, encourage them to state their age and the date of their birthday. Look for similarities, and suggest that the children sort the badges into sets (the same shape, colour, number...)

As the children suggest potential designs for their own badges, encourage them to name the materials they want to use. What size and shape will they choose? What colour number do they want? Are they going to use pictures or patterns to decorate their badges?

Show the children how the Velcro can be used to 'stick on' their badges. Help each child to fix the finished badge to a place of their choice, and then evaluate all the badges. Which ones are most successful and why?

Follow-up activity

Invite the children to invent their own means of fixing a card badge to clothing (avoid causing any damage to their own clothes by using old clothes from the dressing-up box). Offer them string, thick wool, ribbons, paper-clips, treasury tags, hairclips, pipe-cleaners and small bulldog clips. Ask them to show their invention to the group and describe its construction. Assess the advantages and disadvantages of each design.

CHAPTER 3
WHO SHARES MY HOME?

The people with whom young children live are an important focus in their daily lives, and can provide the theme of many exciting activities. However, exploring families can require a delicate approach. Make sure that the activities allow for a diversity of family types, and avoid implying that some families are 'more normal' than others.

FAMILY PORTRAITS

Objective

Art – To draw a family portrait.

Group size

Up to six children.

What you need

Photographs of the children's families, white cartridge paper, six black drawing pens, water in small pots, six thin brushes.

What to do

Ask each child to name and describe each person in their family photograph. Help the child to establish the relationships between them (parents, uncles and aunts, grandparents and so on).

Give each child a piece of white paper and a pen, and ask them to draw a large picture of their family group. Encourage them to draw their own arrangement of the group, and refer them to the photographs for details of physical appearance and clothing. Allow them to include other members of their family even if they do not appear in the photograph. For example, they may have a new baby sister or Mummy may have been taking the photograph.

Encourage the children to use the pens to create dark areas by colouring in or shading. When they have finished their drawing, invite them to use the brush to add a small amount of water to selected areas, blurring the lines. Label and display the finished pictures.

Discussion

Encourage the children to talk about the physical appearance of each person in their photograph. Who's the tallest or shortest? Which people have long hair? What clothes are they wearing? Such questions will help children to include more details in their drawings.

Talk about the sort of marks and lines which can be made with the pens. More mature children could be encouraged to experiment on a piece of scrap paper. Can they make long curved lines or short spiky ones for hair? Where will they use thick or thin lines? Which areas will they colour in or shade? Talk about what happens when water is added to the ink, and the need to use it selectively.

When the pictures are displayed, ask each child to talk about their family portrait to the rest of the group.

Follow-up activity

Write a group poem about a relative. Acting as scribe, ask each child to contribute a line to the poem. For example, a poem about dads might include:

> *'Dads... make castles with Lego,*
> *play ball in the garden,*
> *read stories at night,*
> *put plasters on cuts,*
> *sometimes get cross*
> *and give cuddles in bed.'*

PUPPET FAMILIES

Objective

Technology – To make a simple puppet.

Group size

Up to six children.

What you need

Six small cardboard tubes (various heights), six small pieces of white card, six bendy straws, pencils, wax crayons, felt-tipped pens, a stapler, a variety of collage materials (paper, fabric, wool and so on), PVA adhesive, glue sticks, adhesive tape, six pairs of scissors.

What to do

Explain that the group is going to make a puppet family from a collection of cardboard tubes. Help each child decide which member of the family to make. More experienced children could draw their designs beforehand and list the materials needed. The construction method is illustrated below.

Show the cardboard tubes to the children, then ask them to choose one of an appropriate height to represent their character. Allow them to choose a piece of fabric or paper to stick on to the tube as a covering.

Give each child a piece of white card and ask them to fold it in half. Suggest they draw the shape of the head and neck on one half and cut it out (cutting through both halves of the card, but leaving a hinge at the top to join the two pieces). Very young children may need help with this.

Invite the children to use any of the drawing media or collage materials to add features to the heads. When these are completed, help staple the head to the cardboard tube body. Then suggest the children add other features (arms, legs) or items of clothing (shoes, buttons, scarves, belts, aprons, cloaks) to the figure, using any of the materials available.

When the puppet is completed, attach a bendy straw to its back as a means of control (as shown below). When the adhesive has dried, allow the children a period of free play with their puppets.

Discussion

Emphasise the need to make the features and clothing of the puppet reflect the chosen family member. Talk about which materials are suitable for various purposes. Which would be best for hair or a beard?

Evaluate how well the puppets work. What actions can the children make their puppets perform – walking, jumping, standing on their heads? What are the limitations of this design? How could any difficulties be overcome? Encourage the children to give the puppet an appropriate voice for talking with other members of the family.

Follow-up activities

✧ Challenge the children to make up a short play, using their puppet family, to present to the rest of the group.
✧ Ask them to write or dictate a profile of their puppet – age, sex, position in family, likes and dislikes, favourite activity.
✧ Make a collection of different types of puppet and discuss their design.

Cut along dotted line.

1. Draw head and neck shape on folded card and cut out.

2. Add features and clothing to body.

3. Tape straw to back.

straw

FAMILY TREASURE HUNT

Objective

Geography — To find members of a family, using symbols for familiar features of the immediate environment.

Group size

Up to six children.

What you need

Four pieces of card, felt-tipped pens, adhesive plastic film, a Chinagraph pencil, four small toys to represent the family (play people, small dolls or teddies).

Preparation

Hide the four toys in various places without the children seeing — this activity could take place inside or outside, depending upon the weather. How well you conceal the toys should depend upon the age and experience of the children.

On each piece of card, draw a simple picture to give a clue as to where each toy is hidden. Cover each card with adhesive plastic film. Use the Chinagraph pencil to label the cards 1st, 2nd, 3rd and 4th, and write the name of the appropriate family member on each card (see illustration).

What to do

Explain to the children that the toy family have got lost and their task is to find them. Show them each card in turn. Explain that the numbers on the cards show the order in which they must look for the four toys. Ask them to identify the picture symbol for the place where the toy is hidden, and help them to read the name of the family member.

Mix up the cards, then ask the children to sequence them correctly. Can the children work together to find the toys in the correct order? Adult supervision may be needed, depending on the age and ability of the children. When the children return with the toys, ask them to sequence the cards and place the correct toy on top.

Repeat the activity by changing the numbers and names of family members to make a different treasure hunt (Chinagraph pencil rubs off easily). If the children can find four family members easily, extend the number of cards and toys.

Discussion

Make sure the children understand the ordinal aspect of numbers by asking them to form a line and call out their respective positions. Let them try to identify the place pictured on each card and then point to each place as it is recognised.

As the children search, bring as much positional vocabulary (behind, in between, on top, under, in front, beside) into the conversation as possible. Ask the children to describe the place where they are searching, and to remember the exact position of the toy when it is found.

At the end, discuss how well the children have sequenced the cards, whether they have matched the correct family member to each card and if they can describe exactly where he or she was found.

Follow-up activities

✧ Improve the children's positional vocabulary by asking them to draw and describe precisely each toy's position.
✧ Older children could design their own treasure hunt, inventing new picture symbols to represent other places in their environment.

TEDDY BEAR FAMILY TREE

Objective
History – To introduce the idea of a family tree.

Group size
Up to six children.

What you need
A collection of teddy bears (up to ten), a large piece of sugar paper, black felt-tipped pens, small pieces of white cartridge paper, pencils, wax crayons, glue sticks.

What to do
Put the large piece of sugar paper on the floor and gather the children around the bottom end of the paper. Choose one of the small teddy bears and give her a name. Place her at the bottom of the paper and write her name on it with the pen. Explain to the children that they are going to help invent a family for her, using the other teddies.

Ask each child in turn to help make decisions about the bear's family. Allow a child to choose another teddy, give it a name and place it on the paper beside the original teddy. Write the name on the paper below the teddy. Invite two other children to choose and name two teddies to represent parents. Draw family tree lines on the paper and show the children where to place the parents. Write in their names. Are the parents going to have any brothers or sisters? Invite individual children to choose and name teddies to represent these and show them where to place the

teddies on the paper, writing in their names. Restrict the number of brothers and sisters to one or two. More mature children may be capable of adding another generation involving grandparents.

When the family tree is complete, make a permanent record by asking each child to draw a picture of the teddy they chose on a small piece of paper. Remove the real teddies and stick the small pictures in their place. Display the family tree picture and repeat the activity with several other groups of children. Compare the family trees.

Discussion
As the teddies are being chosen and placed on to the paper, talk about the relationships involved (daughter, sister, brother, mum, dad, uncle, aunt). Check that the children have understood by asking them to point to the teddy representing the first bear's mum, brother or uncle.

Encourage the children to relate the fictional teddy family to their own family, but be sensitive to children who do not wish to make a contribution. Also, be aware of children who may have experienced a divorce or the death of a relative and so may not live with both parents or siblings.

Follow-up activities
✧ Encourage parents and children to make their own family tree, but don't make it compulsory. Show the parents the pictorial family tree of teddy bears and suggest that they could do the same at home, substituting photographs or drawings of their own family.
✧ Make family trees for families in popular stories such as 'The Three Bears', or the 'Alfie' or 'My Naughty Little Sister' stories by Shirley Hughes and Dorothy Edwards respectively.

SAFELY HOME

Objective

English — A pre-handwriting activity to improve visual discrimination and hand-eye co-ordination. It also offers opportunities to extend speaking and listening skills by giving and receiving instructions.

Group size

Up to six children.

What you need

A carpeted area of a room, a large piece of white paper, a black felt-tipped pen, two dolls (one large and one small), two teddy bears (one large and one small), pencils, crayons, photocopiable sheet 90.

Preparation

Put the large piece of white paper on the floor in the carpeted area. Place the large teddy bear and doll at one edge of the paper and the small teddy bear and doll at the opposite edge. Use the black felt-tipped pen to draw a large simple maze connecting the toys, similar to that on the photocopiable sheet. Make sure the pathways are large enough for the children to 'walk' the small teddy bear and doll along. Also, make sure there are several alternative pathways.

What to do

Gather the children round the maze, making sure they can all see it easily. Make up a story in which the small teddy bear and doll have each become separated from a parent while out walking in the woods, playing in the park or on a shopping trip. Explain that the young toys are very sad because they cannot find their parents.

Make sure that the children realise which toy matches with which parent, then ask them to look carefully at the maze to find a pathway from the child to the adult. Suggest that a volunteer tries to 'walk' the small teddy bear to the parent, and repeat this with the small doll.

Discussion

Encourage the children to give each teddy bear and doll a name. Have any of the children ever been lost? Can the children understand how the toys feel and describe these feelings?

Challenge the children to find alternative routes for each toy to the matching adult. Which is the longest or shortest route? Can one child give instructions to another to 'walk' one of the toys along a route, using simple directional language such as forwards, backwards, sideways? Discuss the toys' emotions when they are reunited.

Use this opportunity to talk about what children should do if they get lost, and the problems of 'stranger danger'.

Follow-up activity

Use the photocopiable sheet on page 90 to consolidate this activity. Ask the children to use a pencil to draw in the route for each toy, making sure their pencil line does not bump into the edges of the pathway. Invite them to colour in the pictures. Older children could be challenged to draw their own maze and offer it to a friend to find the way through.

DRESSING DOLL FAMILY

Objective

Mathematics — A measuring activity to match both objects and pictures according to size.

Group size

Up to six children.

What you need

Three dolls (each obviously different in size from the others), clothing for each doll, photocopiable sheet 91, pencils, crayons.

What to do

Take the clothes off each of the dolls, then show the dolls to the children. Invite them to give the dolls names and suggest the family relationships between them — for example, a mother and two daughters or a mother, son and grandmother. Make up a story in which the dolls' clothes have become muddled up, and ask the children to work in pairs to dress one of the dolls in the correct clothing. Repeat the activity by swapping the dolls between pairs.

Discussion

Talk with the children about each item of clothing. What is it called? Which part of the body does it go on to? What colour is it? How does it fasten? Would it only be worn by a girl? What material is it made of? Is it suitable for hot or cold weather?

Encourage the children to predict which clothes will fit their dolls before they try them on. Use comparative vocabulary such as too big, smaller than, not big enough, largest and so on. Discuss the order in which the clothes should be put on. Is it better to put trousers on before underwear? Is one particular item of clothing more difficult to put on than the rest? Ask the children to compare dressing the dolls with dressing themselves at home or at PE time. What do the children find most difficult and why?

Follow-up activities

✧ Give the children photocopiable sheet 91. Make sure that the children recognise each item of clothing, and ask them to draw a line to match each item of clothing to the correct part of the body for each doll. Remind them to take size into account when allocating the clothing. Invite them to colour in the pictures.

✧ Ask older children to draw another item of clothing (in three appropriate sizes) for the dolls.

BIRTHDAYS

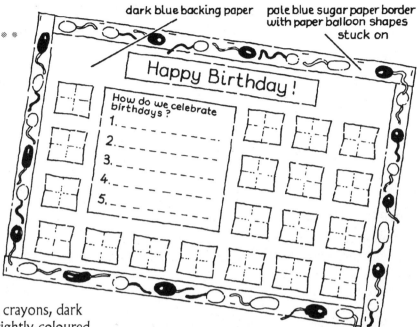

dark blue backing paper

pale blue sugar paper border with paper balloon shapes stuck on

Objective

RE — To share ways of celebrating birthdays within families.

Group size

Any size for the initial discussion, but small groups (up to six) for recording.

What you need

Pale blue sugar paper, a black felt-tipped pen, small pieces of white drawing paper, pencils, wax crayons, dark blue backing paper, a variety of brightly-coloured papers, PVA adhesive, glue sticks, scissors, coloured wool, a stapler.

child's drawings on white paper folded in four

What to do

Pin a large piece of pale blue sugar paper near to the carpet area, where it can easily be seen. Ask the children 'How do we celebrate birthdays?' and write this as a heading at the top of the paper. Write a list of the children's ideas on the paper: get birthday cards, sing 'Happy Birthday', have parties, visit relatives, get presents, go on outings, wear special clothes, eat birthday cakes, play special games, decorate home with balloons, and so on. Then talk with the children in small groups about how different members of their families celebrate their own birthdays. Do siblings, parents and grandparents all celebrate in the same way? Use the list as a focus for discussion.

Give each child a square piece of white paper and fold it into four. In the top left quarter, ask the children to draw and colour a picture of themselves celebrating their birthday. Under this picture, ask them to provide (by dictating) one or two sentences to describe what is happening. In the other spaces on the paper, invite the children to draw a picture of the family celebrating another member's birthday together, with a brief description.

Cover a display board with dark blue paper and write a 'Happy Birthday' label on pale blue sugar paper. Staple the list, the label and the children's pictures on to the display board. Now cut some pale blue sugar paper into strips to form a border

around the display. Invite the children to cut coloured balloon shapes from a variety of papers and stick these on to the border strips. Suggest that they stick on coloured wool to add a string to each balloon. Staple the balloon border around the edge of the display (see illustration).

Discussion

During discussion, try to draw out the similarities and differences between ways of celebrating birthdays. Initially, ask the children to compare how their peers celebrate and then to look at relatives of different ages. Which features are common to all (birthday cards and presents)? What are the differences between age groups? Help the children to realise that there are many different ways of celebrating birthdays, but each one marks an important landmark in life.

Follow-up activities

◇ Make a display to show the month in which each child was born.
◇ Sing 'The birthday song' in the Resources section on page 68.

KEEP BABY SAFE

Objective

Science — To understand that safety is important to the well-being of babies.

Group size

Up to six children.

What you need

A set of objects which are safe for a baby (baby toys, cloth books, a plastic feeding bottle, reins, a Babygro, a car seat), a set of objects which are unsafe for a baby (scissors, a knife, a glass bottle, clothing with unsafe decoration such as ribbons, toys with small parts, a candle, an empty medicine bottle), two set rings, two labels (one marked 'safe' in green, one marked 'unsafe' in red), a baby doll, sugar paper in different colours, a choice of colouring media (felt-tipped pens, wax crayons, coloured pencils), an example of a safety poster.

What to do

Show the children the baby doll and talk about the need to care for her by keeping her away from harm. Put the two set rings on the floor, adding the 'safe' label to one and the 'unsafe' label to the other and explaining what the labels mean. Place the baby doll next to the 'safe' set ring to help the children distinguish the sets. Show the children the collection of objects and ask them to take turns to choose an object and place it in the correct set.

If the children are unfamiliar with posters, show them an example and discuss its design. Then suggest the children design their own 'Keep Baby Safe' posters. Young children can discuss their potential designs, while older children can do preliminary drawings. Invite the children to choose from the selection of paper and drawing media.

Display the baby doll, the two sets of objects and the finished posters.

Discussion

Talk about each object as it is placed in its set. What is it? Is it safe or unsafe? Why? Widen the discussion by asking the children to suggest other hazards to babies, such as water, electricity and so on. Stress the need for adults and older children to be responsible for the safety of babies.

When discussing the poster, draw attention to the need for bold print, eye-catching colours and large pictures. Encourage the children to take account of this when designing their own posters. Refer them back to the collection of objects for ideas. An adult could act as scribe if necessary. Ask the children to evaluate the finished posters. Which ones are most successful and why?

Follow-up activities

✧ Set up a nursery area to encourage role-play. Include baby dolls, a pram or buggy, a cot, a baby bath, baby clothes, talcum powder, nappies, baby wipes, a changing mat, feeding bottles, toys and books. Emphasise the need to keep the baby safe by adding safety equipment such as reins, stair-gates and fireguards. Sometimes place an 'unsafe' object, such as scissors, somewhere in the nursery to see if the children notice.

✧ Read the poem 'Inside' in the Resources section on page 77.

CHAPTER 4
WHAT CAN I DO?

Young children are proud of their increasing physical and intellectual achievements. Being able to do up their own coat buttons or write their own names are important goals which children are eager to share with those around them. The activities in this chapter use these skills as a basis for developing work in all areas of the curriculum.

'I CAN' POEM

Objective

English — To listen to a poem and respond by writing a new poem.

Group size

Up to six children.

What you need

The 'I can' poem on page 76 of the Resources section, white paper, felt-tipped pens, Blu-tack, coloured sugar paper, pencils, wax crayons.

What to do

Read the poem aloud and discuss it with the children, identifying all the achievements mentioned in it. Repeat the poem once or twice, encouraging the children to join in and add actions. If the children are mature enough, read through the poem slowly and ask them to identify all the rhyming words.

Explain that the children are going to write their own 'I can' poem. Place a large sheet of white paper where everyone in the group can see it easily. Ask the children to think of and say all the things they can do, while you list their ideas on the paper.

Place a second large sheet of paper beside the first and write 'I can...' as a title. Ask each child in turn to choose an idea from the list (or suggest a new one) and make up a short sentence for the poem. There is no need for the poem to rhyme. Read through the resulting poem several times, improving the quality of the vocabulary and helping the children to identify unnecessary words.

When a final version has been agreed, write out the poem with each line on a separate piece of paper. Older children could write for themselves, while an adult could act as scribe for younger children. Use Blu-tack to mount the poem on to coloured sugar paper. Ask each child to draw and colour a small picture to illustrate their line, and use these to decorate the poem.

Recite the poem and encourage the children to devise actions to accompany it. Also invite a child to change the order of the lines by moving the paper strips around.

Discussion

Although many young children can identify rhymes, it is very difficult for them to create a rhyming poem; so avoid this unless they are very keen and proficient. When suggesting initial ideas, encourage the children to think of new ideas and not simply to repeat those in the poem they have heard.

The length of time spent on improving the poem will depend on the concentration span of the group. It is important for them to see that initial ideas can be altered, but avoid making this a chore.

Follow-up activity

Make individual achievement records based on activities undertaken at playgroup or school. Ask each child to choose a coloured gummed circle and dictate a (different) achievement to be written on the circle, then stuck to a caterpillar's head.

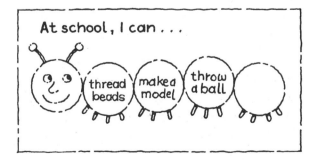

At school, I can . . .
thread beads / make a model / throw a ball

SAND TIMER CHALLENGES

* *

Objective

Mathematics – To develop an awareness of the passing of one minute.

Group size

Up to six children.

What you need

Four small tables, three one-minute sand timers, simple activity equipment such as beads and laces, pegs and peg boards, shape posting toys, simple puzzles, a simple record form (see Figure 1), pencils, a plastic box, a paper 'banner', felt-tipped pens, an adult to supervise.

Figure 1

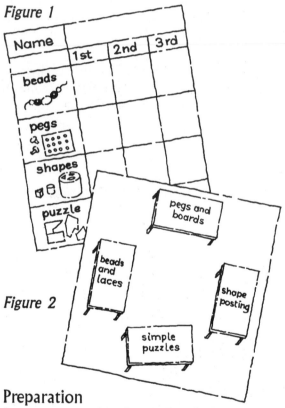

Figure 2

Preparation

Set up an area for the challenges to take place. Arrange the four small tables in an open square (see Figure 2) that is easy to get into or out of. Write 'Sand timer challenges' on the paper banner and display it near to the area. Put one sand timer and one activity on each table. Put the record forms and pencils in the plastic box and place them at one end of one of the tables.

What to do

Show the children how the sand timer works. Invite a child to hold the sand timer and watch the sand as it falls through. Tell them to say 'stop' when it has all passed through. Encourage the others to do a simple activity (clap or nod their heads) during this time. Repeat this until you are sure the children can use the sand timer competently.

Explain what the children have to do for each activity (threading beads, putting pegs in a board, posting shapes and completing a puzzle). Suggest that they work in pairs, with one child supervising the sand timer while the other undertakes an activity of their choice. When the minute has passed, the child needs to complete the record sheet by counting the number of correctly used beads, pegs, shapes or pieces of joined-up puzzle and writing this in the appropriate column. Very young children will need adult help with the counting and recording. The children then swap places and repeat the activity.

Encourage the children to try each activity more than once, so that they can compare their own efforts; but limit the number of tries to three or four. Allow the children the freedom to choose the number and type of activities they attempt.

Discussion

Help the children to realise that the comparisons between their scores will not be fair unless the sand timer is used correctly. Encourage them to compare their own efforts, rather than entering into competition with others. Which was their best attempt? Can they provide an explanation for this? Did they find some activities easier than others? Try to assess whether they are beginning to develop an understanding of 'one minute' as a period of time by asking them to suggest other activities which could be completed in one minute. For example, could they have a bath, travel to school or sing a song?

Follow-up activity

Invite the children to create their own challenges and substitute them for those tried already. For example, they might think of building with construction toys, such as Duplo or sticklebricks, or dressing a doll. With experience, the children can also be asked to predict the results before undertaking the activity.

BEAN BAGS

❋ ❋

Objective

PE – To explore ways of moving bean bags.

Group size

Up to six children.

What you need

Six bean bags, a large open space, a record sheet as shown in Figure 1, pencils.

What to do

Ask each child to choose a bean bag and then to find five different ways of making it travel a short distance.

Give each child a pencil and a record sheet (see Figure 1) and suggest they record each method after they have devised it. Depending on the age of the children, an adult could act as scribe or the children could draw pictures or write brief descriptions. Children who are enjoying the activity and think they can find more ways to move the bean bag could continue their recording on the reverse side of the sheet.

Discussion

If the children are unfamiliar with bean bags, it is useful to ask them to describe the bags in detail (shape, size, colour, texture, smell, weight) before beginning the activity.

Encourage the children to discover their own methods of moving the bean bag, rather than copying each other. Their suggestions might include balancing it on part of their own body (head, neck, shoulder, elbow, back of hand, knee, foot) while moving, throwing it, kicking it, sliding it along the ground or pushing it along the ground with different parts of their body.

Allow a short time for each child to show and describe the ideas they have recorded on the sheet to the other members of the group. Highlight similarities and differences in their methods.

Follow-up activities

✧ Suggest that the children choose one of their methods for moving the bean bag and paint or draw a picture of themselves using it. Combine the pictures to make a class frieze.
✧ Complete the photocopiable sheet on page 92.
✧ Repeat the activity, but with a different piece of small apparatus such as a ball or hoop.

Figure 1

With a bean bag, I can . . . . .

MY HANDS

Objective

Science — To increase awareness of the importance of hands in daily life.

Group size

Up to six children.

What you need

A scarf, a book, a construction toy, a hat, a plastic beaker, white paper, pencils, crayons, coloured card, finger paints, PVA adhesive, glue sticks.

Preparation

Place the book, construction toy, hat and beaker on a table within easy reach of the group. Tie the hands of one child behind her back using the scarf, and invite her to try to use the items on the table. Let the others take a turn. Use this activity to highlight how difficult life would be without hands. Ask the children to name as many activities as possible for which we use our hands.

What to do

Explain that each child is going to make a zigzag book about hands. Give them each four small pieces of white paper, and ask them to draw and colour in pictures of themselves using their hands in different ways. Suggest that they dictate or write a sentence describing their actions on four separate small pieces of paper.

Fold strips of coloured card into zigzags (one strip per child). This is probably best done by an adult. Tell the children to use the finger paints to make handprints on their strip of card and when the paints are dry, to stick the pictures and text on to the pages to form a book. Write the title and name of the author on small pieces of white paper and stick these on to the front cover (see below).

Encourage each child to read their finished zigzag book to the group, and then display them all for others to read.

Discussion

Inspire ideas by talking about the ways in which we use our hands in everyday life. Name parts of the hand and discuss which parts are involved in various hand actions.

Focus the children's attention on the importance of their hands in performing the printing activity. Could they put on aprons or mix paints without using their hands? Talk about the prints made by their hands, and look for lines both on the prints and on the skin of their hands. When discussing the finished books, compare both the handprints and the ideas written on the pages. How are one child's handprints different from another's?

Count the number of different activities involving hands which have been identified in the books.

Follow-up activities

✧ Teach the children several simple finger and hand rhymes. Encourage them to identify the various movements their hands and fingers are making.
✧ Sing the song 'I use my hands' in the Resources section on page 72.

MARK-MAKING CHALLENGE

Objective

Art – To select a tool and explore the range of marks it can make.

Group size

Up to six children.

What you need

Play dough, Plasticine or clay (only one of these is needed), three rolling pins, a small collection of tools (a plastic or wooden modelling tool, a toothbrush, a comb, a glue stick, a twig, a fir cone, a screw), small pieces of card, felt-tipped pens, a small table covered in paper or fabric for display.

What to do

Invite the children to take a piece of play dough (or Plasticine, or clay) and use a rolling pin to roll it flat. Show them the tools, naming each one; then ask the children to choose one tool and press it into their play dough to find out how many different marks it will make.

Suggest that they look around the room for a tool of their own (checking with an adult before using it) and repeat the activity on a second piece of play dough. Then ask the children to choose a piece of play dough to put on display, marking their initials on the underside.

Display the play dough pieces on the small table, and place the corresponding tool somewhere on the table (but not necessarily next to the play dough piece). Make a card label for each piece of play dough, with the name of the child who marked it on one side and a picture of the tool used on the reverse. Place the correct label, with the name facing upwards, next to each piece. Invite the children to guess which tool made the marks on each piece of play dough and then find out if they are right by turning over the card.

Discussion

Encourage the children to describe the feel of the play dough and the effect the rolling pin has on it. As they work with their chosen tool, encourage them to experiment with all parts of it and describe the marks produced.

Compare the finished pieces of play dough. How many different marks were produced with each tool? Are any marks the same? Which tool made the most marks? Which piece of play dough do the children prefer and why?

Follow-up activity

Repeat the activity using a different medium, such as paint, and a different range of tools.

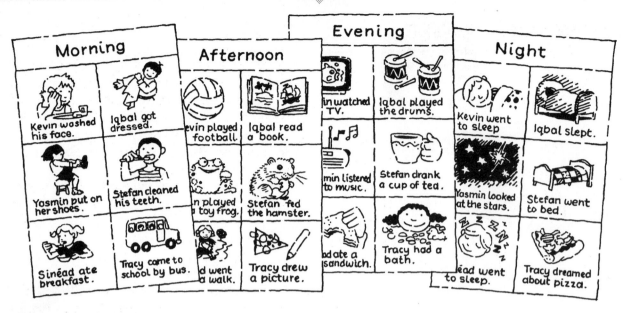

OUR DAY

Objective

History — To introduce vocabulary in order to describe broad periods of time during the day (morning, afternoon, evening, night) and to sequence these correctly.

Group size

Up to six children.

What you need

Four large sheets of white paper, felt-tipped pens, a hole punch, a treasury tag, four drawing pins.

Preparation

Label one sheet of paper for each of the time periods: morning, afternoon, evening, night. Then divide each sheet of paper into six large rectangles.

What to do

Talk with the children about the things they did yesterday, reminding them of the date. Ask them what they can remember doing during each of the time periods, and explain that they are going to make a picture diary to show what they did. Show them the four labelled sheets and suggest that they each dictate one activity for each time period. Then ask them to illustrate each sentence using the felt-tipped pens.

Play a game by mixing up the finished sheets and asking individual children to sequence them correctly. Punch a hole through the top of all the sheets, then thread them on to a treasury tag and pin them to a display board. Above the display, add a label 'Our day' with the appropriate day and date (including year). Allow the children free access to look at the picture diary and practise sequencing the pictures.

Discussion

If the children are unfamiliar with the concept of a diary, explain what it is and show them an example. Encourage each child to think of a different activity. Discuss whether the activity is something they do every day, or whether it was specific to yesterday.

As they suggest activities, reinforce the order of the time periods. Talk about which one comes first, second and so on, or what comes before or after the evening.

Follow-up activities

✧ Make a class diary for the week, recording one activity for each day. Draw seven frames (one per day), and at the end of each daily session choose one child to draw a picture of an important activity for that day within the frame. Write a brief sentence underneath to describe the activity. Use the diary to introduce time vocabulary: yesterday, today, tomorrow, days of the week, weekend.
✧ Read the poem 'Bedtime in summer' in the Resources section on page 81.

WORKING TOGETHER

. . . .

Objective

Technology — To build a simple collective model.

Group size

Six to eight children.

What you need

A collection of construction equipment, including a large base board (Duplo, LEGO or any other appropriate construction toy).

What to do

Tell the children to sit in a circle on the carpet, and explain that they are going to work together to build a model. Place the construction equipment in the middle of the circle, then give one child the base board. Ask the child to choose a construction piece, fix it to the base board and say what it is (a house, a box, a bridge...) Then pass the base board on to the next child and invite her to add another piece and name the new structure. Repeat this activity going around the circle.

Discussion

Talk with the children about the construction pieces they choose (colour, size, shape) and where they decide to place them (on top, beside, next to, in between). If appropriate, count the number of pieces that have been used. Each child can put their own interpretation on the developing model, or the group may decide to work towards the same idea (such as a castle or a bus).

Talk about other activities which the children can do collectively. Which do they enjoy most and why?

Follow-up activity

Make some prompt cards to be used with the construction toys. For example, 'Can you build a house [boat, bridge, animal] with ten pieces of Duplo?' Invite the children to choose a card and attempt the task it gives.

BODY SOUNDS

Objective

Music – To explore body sounds and then select and combine some into a simple sequence.

Group size

Up to six children.

What you need

A tape recorder and blank cassette.

What to do

Ask the children to sit in a circle, and explain that they are going to make sounds with their bodies. These could include clapping hands, slapping knees, stamping feet, tapping toes or heels, rubbing hands together, or a whole range of voice sounds. Make a sound yourself and ask the children to join in one at a time as you move around the circle. Repeat this with one or two more body sounds of your own and then ask individuals to suggest other sounds. Introduce the idea of loud and soft sounds and ask the children to identify them.

Extend this activity by making a sequence of body sounds. Demonstrate one or two yourself for the children to copy, and then ask individuals to make up their own for the group to copy. Encourage them to combine loud and soft sounds.

Invite each child to make up a short sequence of body sounds to be recorded on a cassette. Allow them enough time to rehearse before helping them to record the sequence.

Discussion

When the children are making sounds as a group, encourage them to maintain an even rhythm. Talk about the different methods they are using to make sounds. Which sound is loudest or softest? Which sound do they like least or best?

Encourage the children to describe the sound sequence they are making. Which part of the body is being used? How many sounds are being made? Are they loud or soft? Children who are experienced in the use of a tape recorder will be able to work together to record their sound sequences, but very young children will need adult assistance. Discuss the recorded sequences, identifying individual body sounds.

Follow-up activities

✧ Challenge the children to invent body sounds to accompany a short story (such as 'The Little Indian Boy' in the 'Some Special People' section of *This Little Puffin*, published by Young Puffin).
✧ Invent body sounds to accompany songs such as 'We're going on a bear hunt' by Michael Rosen and Helen Oxenbury (Walker).
✧ Read the poem 'Animal sounds we can make' in the Resources section on page 80.

CHAPTER 5
HOW DO I FEEL?

This chapter looks at emotions such as happiness, sadness, anger and fear. Many young children may still be finding it difficult to cope with emotions such as anger and sadness, and may need help to find appropriate ways of expressing these feelings.

CLOWN SHAPES

Objective

Mathematics – To use happy and sad clown faces as a way to reinforce shape recognition.

Group size

Small group of four to six children.

What you need

Photocopiable sheet 93, a Chinagraph pencil, a blank dice, coloured pencils.

Preparation

Make photocopies of the activity sheet and cut them in half (one clown picture is needed per child). On each face of the dice, draw one of five plane shapes (a circle, a semicircle, a triangle, a square or a rectangle), leaving one face blank.

What to do

Allow each child to choose a clown picture. Talk about the expression shown on each one, and identify the plane shapes. Show the children the dice and name the plane shape on each face. Explain that they are going to take turns to throw the dice. Whichever shape lands uppermost on their turn

can then be coloured in on their clown face. If they have already coloured in all of those shapes, or if the blank face of the dice is uppermost, they miss a turn. The first child to colour in all six plane shapes on their clown face is the winner.

Discussion

Ask the children to spot the differences between the two clown faces and explain how we can tell that one clown is happy and the other one is sad. Make sure they can all identify the plane shapes by asking them to point to a circle or a semicircle on their picture. Count the number of circles, and other shapes on each face. Which face has more of each shape?

At the end of the game, ask each child to count the number of shapes they have coloured in. Name each shape that has been left uncoloured.

Follow-up activities

✧ Make up a story to explain why the clown is happy or sad. Tell the stories orally, or write them down in small books shaped like clown faces.

✧ Offer the children gummed paper shapes and ask them each to make a picture of a clown's face, showing an expression of their (individual) choice.

GOOD AND BAD NEWS

Objective

Geography — To learn and understand the composition of home addresses by writing happy and sad letters to family members.

Group size

Up to six children.

What you need

Two sample letters, pencils, pens, crayons, writing paper, envelopes, stamps.

Preparation

Write and post two sample letters to yourself, one containing happy news and the other containing sad news. For example, the happy news could be the birth of a child, a wedding or party invitation, someone asking to visit or someone inviting you on a trip. The sad news could include a close friend or relative moving house, losing a precious possession or having an accident. The envelopes have been correctly addressed and stamped by you, and franked by the Post Office. (You could actually post the letters, or use envelopes from letters already posted.)

What to do

Tell the children that you have received two letters in the morning post, one which made you feel very sad and one which made you happy. Read the letters to the children and ask them to identify the emotion provoked by each. Invite them to describe any occasions when they, or members of their families, have received letters with happy or sad news. Can they think of any other happy or sad news they might receive?

Talk about the conventions of letter writing, using your letters and envelopes as examples. Ask the children to point to the address, stamp and date on the envelopes and the address, date, opening phrase *(Dear . . .)* and closing phrase *(Love from . . .)* on the letters. Suggest the children write a happy or sad letter to someone at home, using the letter-writing materials. An adult can act as scribe for young children. Take the opportunity to draw their attention to the address at the top of the letter and on the envelope.

When the letters are finished and placed in envelopes, mix them up, read out the addresses (but not the names) on the envelopes and ask each child to identify their letter. Take them to post their letters in a post-box. Warn the parents about the arrival of these letters, and encourage them to write back to their children to provide an added dimension to the project.

Discussion

Explain the meaning of each part of the children's addresses: the number or name of the house, the name of the road, the district, the village, town or city, the county and postcode.

Suggest that the children read their finished letter to a friend and ask them to identify whether it contains happy or sad news.

If members of the family reply to the letters, encourage the children to bring in the replies to share with the group.

Follow-up activities

✧ Help the children make a large address book, with all their addresses recorded in alphabetical order. Use the address book for further letter-writing activities, inviting the children to find a friend's address and write to them.
✧ Talk about the person who delivers the post and the work of the Post Office.

THE HAPPIEST DAY OF MY LIFE

* *

Objective

History – To describe an important personal event from the past.

Group size

Up to six children.

What you need

A photograph of an important event (or a happy time) in your life, white drawing paper, pencils, crayons, sugar paper, PVA adhesive, glue sticks, a stapler (for the book).

What to do

Show the children the photograph and tell them it portrays a happy day in your life. Ask them to describe what they can see in the photograph. Can they deduce what the situation or event is? Ask each child to think of the happiest day in their life and to describe it to the group. The occasions might include a birthday, a wedding or the birth of a sibling, a religious or cultural celebration (Diwali, Christmas or Guy Fawkes' Night), or a special event (a party, outing or holiday).

Suggest each child draws and writes about their happiest day. Stick the pictures and writing on to sugar paper and staple together to make a book called 'The Happiest Day of My Life'.

Discussion

Ask the children for the reasons why this particular time was the happiest day in their life. Who shared the day with them? Help the children to develop their sense of time by trying to relate the 'happiest day' to other events. Was it in winter or summer, this year, last year or a long time ago? How old were they when it happened? Had their baby brother been born? Was it before or after they started playgroup or nursery?

Ask whether they have anything as a record of their day which they could bring in to show the group. For example, they may have a photograph, a greetings card or a ticket and guidebook to a special place.

Follow-up activity

Compile a list of simple, everyday things which can make us happy, such as a hug from Dad, praise from an adult or sharing a game with a friend.

FACE-PAINT FUN

Objective

Technology – To design make-up which reflects an emotion.

Group size

Up to six children.

What you need

Pictures of faces which reflect strong emotions (happy, sad, angry, frightened, surprised – advertisements are often a good source), face-paints, three large mirrors (safety glass or mirror card).

What to do

Talk about the pictures with the children, identifying the emotion displayed in each one. Discuss how our emotions are reflected in our expressions. Compare and contrast the ways that the features of these faces have changed to show different emotions. Invite the children to make their own faces reflect each emotion in turn. Offer them the mirrors to study their faces, and encourage them to look at each other's expressions carefully to see what they can learn.

Ask the children to work in pairs, taking turns to decorate each other's faces with the face-paints. Stress the need to paint a strong emotion. Older children could draw their designs on paper first.

Discussion

How can we tell when someone is happy, sad or surprised? What shapes or lines appear on their face? Which parts of their face move or change in some way? Encourage the children to use the face-paints to draw similar lines and shapes on to their partners' faces. More experienced children may also be capable of using colours symbolically, such as red for anger or blue for sadness.

Allow time to discuss and evaluate the final make-up designs. Which aspects of each design are most successful and why? If possible, photograph each child to provide a record of the designs.

Follow-up activities

✧ Challenge the children to work in pairs and invent a role-play situation which enables them to display the emotions painted on their faces. For example, partners whose faces display anger and sadness may decide to act out an argument over a toy (the angry child taking the toy).
✧ Design and make a mask to illustrate an emotion.
✧ Sing the song 'What's that face?' in the Resources section on page 69.

TONGUE-TWISTERS

Objective

English – To devise tongue-twisters using words with the same initial sound.

Group size

Up to six children.

What you need

A simple drawing of a large face, long pink tongue shapes (made from paper), Blu-Tack, a black felt-tipped pen, an example of a tongue-twister poem (for example, 'Peter Piper').

What to do

Read the tongue-twister poem to the group, and help the children to realise that tongue-twisters involve words with the same sounds. Display the drawing of a face and show them a paper tongue with a tongue-twister already written on it ('Sad Simon sits and sulks' or 'Giggling Glenda gallops round the garden'). Read the tongue-twister to the children and ask them to identify the repeated sounds. Fix the tongue to the mouth on the picture and ask the children to recite the tongue-twister as fast as they can.

Suggest that the group make up their own tongue-twisters for different emotions (happy, angry, miserable, surprised, frightened). Once a satisfactory tongue-twister has been agreed, write it down on one of the tongue shapes. Invite the children to change the tongue-twisters on the face regularly and recite each one quickly.

Discussion

Count the number of words in the tongue-twister which contain the same sound. Which tongue-twister is the most difficult to say and why?

Follow-up activity

Make a collection of other tongue-twister poems.

ANGRY DANCE

Objective

PE – To use movements to represent a story based on the emotion of anger.

Group size

Any size.

What you need

A copy of the story *The Two Giants* by M. Foreman (Hodder & Stoughton), a large open space, a tambourine.

Preparation

Read the story to the children.

What to do

Simplify the story and invite the children to devise movements to accompany the main events. Use the tambourine, in different ways, to accompany the movements and also as a signal to start and stop moving. An example of events and suggested movements is given below.

Discussion

Allow the children to create movements of their own choice, and only offer more detailed suggestions if they lack ideas. Ask three or four children who are responding creatively to demonstrate their movements to others. Encourage them to use the whole floor space and to move in different directions. Talk about whether they are moving gently or strongly, high or low and quickly or slowly.

Follow-up activities

◇ Make paper-plate faces of the giants. On one side use collage to show the giant's happy face, and on the other side make an angry face. Suspend the faces as mobiles.

◇ Read the poem 'How do I feel?' in the Resources section on page 78.

Story	Movement ideas
Boris and Sam (the two giants) walking together.	Holding hands in pairs, treading carefully to avoid trees, and so on.
Boris and Sam paddling in the sea.	Mime paddling and splashing in the water.
Boris and Sam find a shell.	Picking up the shell, admiring it.
Both Boris and Sam want the shell and they begin to argue.	Shake fists, wag fingers, stamp feet (first on the spot and then while moving around).
The sun disappears, the wind and rain begin.	Mime weather conditions.
The waves sweep higher and the giants put on their socks.	Use body to show waves getting higher, and mime putting on socks.
A huge wave washes away the shell and their shoes.	Mime the movement of the water from low to high.
The land is flooded and the giants are each left on separate islands. They are furious.	In pairs, mime throwing stones and then heavy rocks at each other.
Boris sleeps and Sam sneaks up on him (through shallow water).	Tiptoeing carefully from rock to rock in different directions.
Boris wakes and the two giants charge towards each other.	Leaping and striding angrily in a straight line.
Suddenly, they notice they have mixed their socks up and begin to giggle.	Laughing, happy movements (first on the spot and then while moving around).
Neither of them can remember what they were arguing about, and they make friends again.	Walking or skipping happily in pairs in different directions.

HAPPY AND SAD MUSIC

Objective

Music – To listen and respond to short pieces of music.

Group size

Any size.

What you need

Three or four examples of short pieces of music which evoke happy and sad moods, a tape recorder.

What to do

Play each piece of music to the group once to identify whether it is a happy or sad piece of music. Replay each piece two or three times to discover how this mood is evoked. At the end of the discussion, play all the pieces of music through without interruption.

Discussion

Talk with the children about how each piece of music makes them feel. Draw attention to any spontaneous responses such as clapping or tapping hands, body movements or facial expressions.

When replaying the music, encourage the children to describe how each mood is created. Which instruments are being used? Do they hear one sound at a time or lots of sounds together? Identify which sounds are fast or slow, loud or quiet, high or low. Are some sounds longer or shorter? Have periods of silence been used? Compare and contrast the happy pieces of music with the sad ones.

Follow-up activity

Ask the children to work in pairs to compose their own short piece of music to reflect an emotion of their choice. Offer them a selection of percussion instruments (wood block, tambourine, claves, castanets, cymbal, guiro, drum, Indian bells, jingle bells, maracas, triangle) and a xylophone or glockenspiel. When they are satisfied with their composition, record it on tape. Replay all the final pieces to the whole group and evaluate the results. Can the children identify the emotions expressed in the music?

TUNNEL OF FEAR

Objective

RE – To identify the causes of fear.

Group size

Any size.

What you need

A large sheet of paper, a felt-tipped pen, a cuboid-shaped cardboard box (large enough for a child to crawl through) or a plastic play tunnel, paper, paints, scissors, adhesive tape, string.

What to do

Talk about things which make you afraid and then ask the children to reveal the things which frighten them. As they talk, list the things they fear on the large sheet of paper. Once the list is complete, tell the children they are going to make a tunnel in which all these frightening things are hiding.

Paint the outside of the cardboard box black and label it the 'Tunnel of Fear'. Ask individual children to paint pictures or models of the frightening things and put them inside the tunnel. Suggest they also bring in plastic toys (spiders, snakes, monsters) and suspend them as mobiles inside the tunnel. Tick each item on the list as it is put in the tunnel.

Allow small groups of children to play with the tunnel and its contents. Make sure the children understand this activity is voluntary, so that no child is forced to use the tunnel if they are unhappy doing so.

Discussion

When compiling the list of frightening things, ask the children to describe exactly what frightens them and why. Help them to realise that others have similar fears by identifying all those in the group who are afraid of fire or the dark. Talk to the children about how they feel when they are afraid, and what they can do to reduce their anxiety. Try to put irrational fears into perspective. Can spiders really hurt you? Do monsters really exist?

Continue this dialogue with the children as they paint pictures, make models and collect objects to go inside the tunnel. Listen to the children's conversations as they play with the tunnel, since these are often very revealing and can lead to further discussions. Talk with any children who are hesitant about playing in the tunnel. Identify exactly what it is that they dislike, and ask the others to suggest ways of overcoming any fears. For example, would it help to play in the tunnel with a friend, take in a torch or temporarily remove a picture, model or object? Help the children to respect the fears of others while trying to help them overcome these fears.

Follow-up activities

✧ Read stories involving characters who are afraid: for example, *The Owl Who Was Afraid of the Dark* by Jill Tomlinson (Methuen), *Can't You Sleep, Little Bear?* by Martin Waddell (Walker) or *The Monster Bed* by Jeanne Willis and Susan Varley (Andersen Press).

✧ Adapt the song 'Who's Afraid of the Big Bad Wolf?' to the fears suggested by the group. For example, 'Who's afraid of . . . the dark at night [spiders in the bath, shadows on the wall . . .]?'

CHAPTER 6
HOW CAN I LOOK AFTER MYSELF?

Throughout the early years, young children are becoming increasingly independent and are eager to assume responsibility for themselves. This chapter deals with simple health education matters, and is intended to show children how they can look after themselves.

EAT MORE FRUIT

Objective

Mathematics — To make a tally of favourite fruits.

Group size

Any size.

What you need

A selection of real fruits, a knife, small plates, beads, laces, small pieces of card, a hole punch, felt-tipped pens.

What to do

Show the group the selection of fruits and allow the children to handle them. How many of them can they name? Encourage the children to use their senses to explore the fruits. Cut the fruits in half and let the children compare and contrast the inside with the outside. Cut them into small pieces and invite the children to taste each fruit. Talk about the importance of hygiene, and watch out for any children who may be allergic to certain fruits. Discuss the health benefits of eating fresh fruit.

Draw and colour a picture of each fruit on a small piece of card, and punch a hole through each card. Thread a lace through the hole and tie a knot in one end, so the card will not fall off. Ask each child which fruit tastes the best, then tell them to

choose a bead and thread it on to the lace attached to the picture of their favourite fruit. Compare the numbers of beads on the laces to discover the most or least popular fruit. Put the fruits in order from the least to the most popular.

Discussion

Encourage the children to describe the colour, shape, texture and smell of each fruit; sort the fruits into sets according to colour, size or shape; and find words to describe the taste of each fruit. Do the children know why eating fruit is 'good for you'? How often do they eat fruit? Can they justify their likes and dislikes?

Ask questions about the bead tally. Do more children like bananas or apples best? How many more children like grapes than like melon best? Do any fruits have the same tally?

Follow-up activities

◇ Make a fruit alphabet. Draw an alphabet frieze and find a fruit which begins with each letter. Draw and label a picture of each fruit and stick it under each letter with Blu-Tack. Place some of the pictures under the wrong letters and ask the children to spot what's wrong.

◇ Reinforce one-to-one correspondence by using the photocopiable activity sheet on page 94.

APRICOT MILKSHAKE

Objective

Science – To make a healthy drink.

Group size

Up to six children.

What you need

Ingredients: a 4llg tin of unsweetened apricot halves in fruit juice, 4 tablespoons natural yoghurt, 600ml milk, cornflakes for decoration.
Equipment: aprons, a tin opener, a tablespoon, a jug, a glass bowl, 6 knives, 6 small plates, 6 forks, a blender or food processor, 6 glasses, 6 straws.

What to do

Make sure the children wash their hands and put on clean aprons before starting this activity. Open the tin of apricot halves and tip them into the glass bowl, along with the fruit juice. Give each child a small plate and a knife and fork, then share the apricot halves out among the children. (Leave the liquid in the bowl.) Ask them to chop the apricot halves into small pieces and then mash them with the fork.

Tip the mashed apricot back into the bowl with the fruit juice. Add the yoghurt and allow the children to take turns to whisk the mixture. Add the milk and continue to whisk. Then pour the mixture into a blender or food processor and blend for a minute or two.

Pour the milkshake into the glasses and sprinkle a few cornflakes on top of each for decoration. Give each child a glass and a straw.

Discussion

Talk about the importance of milk in a healthy diet. What other ingredient in this recipe is made from milk? Describe the colour, shape, size, texture and smell of the apricot halves. Count the number of halves and ask the children how many whole apricots are in the tin. Point out that some tinned fruits contain a lot of added sugar, but that these are unsweetened.

Describe the changes in the apricots as they are cut and mashed and other ingredients are added. What changes occur through whisking or blending? Taste and describe one or two dry cornflakes. Do they float or sink on the milk shake? After a few minutes, describe how they have changed. Will the cornflakes pass through the straw?

Follow-up activities

✧ Give the children a copy of activity sheet 95. Talk about each picture and relate it to making the milkshake. Ask the children to cut out the pictures and then stick them on to another sheet of paper to show the correct sequence for making the milkshake. With very young children, ask them to place the pictures on to the sheet and then check the sequence before sticking them down.
✧ Invite the children to find items to include in a display of products made from milk.

WASH YOUR HANDS

Objective

Science — To introduce the concept of hygiene and explore the simple properties of soap.

Group size

Six children.

What you need

A water tray, protective clothing, paper towels, four bars of soap in the same colour, three bars of soap in different colours.

What to do

Discuss the importance of washing regularly, then gather the children around the water tray. Ask them to work in pairs. Give each pair a bar of soap in the same colour, and ask them to describe it (appearance, feel, smell) in its dry state. Then ask them to place their bar of soap in the water tray, leave it for a few minutes and describe what happens to it. Use the spare dry bar of soap for comparison with the wet soaps.

Invite the children to use the bars of soap to make a bubbly lather on their hands. Ask them to describe the colour of the bubbles. Allow them to repeat the activity with the different-coloured soaps, predicting and then testing to see what colour the bubbles are.

Discussion

Talk about when the children should wash their hands (after going to the toilet, before eating, after a messy activity).

When comparing the wet and dry soaps, ask the children to describe any changes in colour, smell or texture. What happens to the water around the soap?

Do the children think different-coloured soaps will produce different-coloured bubbles? Encourage them to guess before they make the lather.

Follow-up activities

✧ Design a sign to remind everyone to wash their hands.
✧ Put items associated with hygiene near the water tray for free play activities. Try to include a variety of soaps (solid and liquid), flannels, nail-brushes and different-shaped sponges.

SKELETONS

Objective
Art – To use collage to create a skeleton picture.

Group size
Up to six children.

What you need
A picture or model of a skeleton, dark-coloured sugar paper, white paper, white drinking straws, white matchsticks, white pipe-cleaners, white wool or string, scissors, PVA adhesive, glue sticks.

What to do
Show the children the picture or model of a skeleton and help them to identify the various bones (technical names are not needed). Talk about the way in which bones serve as a framework for our bodies. Emphasise the need to care for bones through a healthy diet, exercise and taking sensible precautions to avoid breaking them.

Invite the children to make skeleton collages on coloured backgrounds of their own choice. Suggest that they choose suitable materials from those provided, and cut or tear them to make appropriate shapes to stick on to the paper. Refer them back to the picture or model for details.

Display the collage pictures alongside the model or picture of a skeleton.

Discussion
As the parts of the skeleton are identified, suggest that the children feel for the bones in their own bodies. Can they feel their ribs, skulls or collar-bones? Count the number of bones in an arm or leg on the model. Why do we need ribs or a skull? What would happen if our bones didn't grow properly or got broken?

As the children make their collages, ask them to justify their choice of materials. Which materials could be used for ribs or finger-bones? Which are flexible or rigid? How can each material be changed (cut, torn, bent) to suit the image of a skeleton? Discuss the type of pose their skeleton will adopt. Will it be waving, jumping or dancing?

Allow time to talk about the finished collages. Which ones do the children prefer and why?

Follow-up activities
◇ Make a collection of bones and study them with magnifying glasses.
◇ Read the *Funnybones* stories by Janet and Allan Ahlberg.

HOOP GAME

Objective

PE – To experience different ways of moving on the floor and develop awareness of the effects of exercise on the body.

Group size

Any size.

What you need

A plastic hoop for each child, a large open space, a tambourine.

What to do

Talk about the need to exercise regularly to ensure that every part of the body is kept in working order. As a warm-up exercise, suggest the children shake every part of their bodies while you shake the tambourine. Ask them to repeat this while moving around.

Give each child a hoop, then tell them to place their hoop on the floor and to stand inside it. Explain that they are going to exercise various parts of their bodies while moving around the hoops without touching them. The sound of the tambourine will give the signal to start moving; when it stops, each child must stand inside a hoop. Tell them which parts of the body they must move each time – such as toes and head, two feet and one arm, one foot and two arms and so on. Repeat the activity, removing a hoop each time and allowing more than one child to stand in a hoop when the signal is given. Continue the activity until only two or three hoops are left.

At the end of the activity, talk about the effects the exercise has had on the children's bodies. How long do these effects last? How do the children think regular exercise affects the body?

Discussion

Naming the parts of the body to be exercised, instead of specifying movements such as hopping or clapping, will enable the children's movement responses to be more open-ended. Praise children who think of unusual ways of moving. Also encourage the children to work co-operatively when standing inside a hoop, trying to fit as many people as possible inside.

At the end of the session, ask the children which parts of their bodies have *not* been exercised. How has exercise changed their bodies? For example, are they tired, hot and sweaty, breathing quickly? Are their hearts beating faster? What would happen if they took no exercise at all?

Follow-up activities

✧ Collect pictures of people involved in a variety of sports and exercise activities such as football, swimming, tennis, aerobics and ice skating. Discuss each activity and describe which parts of the body would be used most.
✧ Read the poem 'Quiet as mice' in the Resources section on page 79.

GO TO SLEEP

* *

Objective

Music — To recognise and use a period of silence in a song.

Group size

Any size.

What you need

A large open space.

What to do

Ask the children to say when periods of silence occur in songs and music — at the beginning, at the end and between verses. Teach the children the following song (to the tune of 'Have you seen the Muffin Man?'):

*I am going to nod my head, nod my head, nod my
head.
But I'm feeling rather tired so now I'll go to sleep.*

Split the group in half and ask one half to sing the song while the other half mime the actions.

Leave a silent pause after the song and then signal (by raising a hand) for the singing group to repeat the song. Emphasise the need for the miming group to remain still and quiet during the period of silence. Repeat the song three or four times.

Change the groups around and alter the words and actions. For example, replace 'nod my head' with 'shake my hands', 'hop up and down', 'skip around' and so on. Invite the children to make up their own words and actions.

Discussion

Ask the children to assess how well they managed to maintain the periods of silence. Did it get easier with practice? Why do they think there are silent breaks in songs?

Talk about the words of the song, relating them to the body's need for sleep. List the effects of having too little sleep, and compare the times that different children go to bed.

Follow-up activities

◇ Ask the children to paint a picture of themselves asleep in bed and to record the time when they went to bed.
◇ Read the poem 'The I-don't-want-to-go-to-bed-dance!' in the Resources section on page 80.

ROAD SAFETY

Objective

Geography — To introduce simple map reading skills through a discussion about road safety.

Group size

Up to six children.

What you need

A plastic or rubber mat with a village or town map marked on it, six toy cars, six toy people.

What to do

Tell the children to sit in a circle around the mat. Ask individuals to point to features on the map (roads, pavements, houses, river, railway line). Point out landmarks and ask the children to name them (garage, shop, park).

Give each child a toy person and ask them to place the toy on to the map in a place where it would be safe to walk. Then ask them to find a safe place on the map to play.

Give each child a toy vehicle and ask them to put the vehicles in a place on the map where vehicles would be found. Invite the children to find a safe place for their toy person to cross the road. Ask individuals to go through the 'Green Cross Code' procedure with their toy person to help them cross the road.

Set challenges for each child. For example, 'Show me the route your person would take from the shop to the park,' or 'Show me the route your vehicle would take from the garage to the railway station.'

Allow a period of free play with the mat and toys.

Discussion

Explain that the mat is a simple type of map. Talk about the way that some colours are used to represent things, such as green for grass and blue for water. Are the pictures of landmarks on this map viewed from above or from the side? How can we tell the difference between the road and the railway track?

Talk about the safe places to walk and play. Are the same places safe for walking and for playing? Emphasise the importance of not playing near traffic. Find the safe places to cross the road on the map and then ask the children to suggest others not shown (traffic lights, a zebra or pelican crossing, a footbridge, an underpass, with a lollipop person).

As the children show you their routes, ask them to describe the landmarks they are passing or to give directions.

Follow-up activities

✧ Invite a lollipop person to visit the group to reinforce safety procedures for crossing the road.
✧ Challenge the children to make their own version of the map by drawing on large sheets of paper. Emphasise the need to include safe places to walk, play and cross the road.
✧ Sing the song 'Look right, look left' in the Resources section on page 74.

JAIRUS' DAUGHTER

Objective

RE – To listen and respond to a story from the Bible and identify people we can trust.

Group size

Any size.

What you need

A simple version of the story of Jairus' daughter (see page 85 of the Resources section), a large sheet of paper, felt-tipped pens, small pieces of drawing paper, pencils, crayons, glue sticks.

What to do

Read the story about Jesus healing Jairus' daughter. Reread the story choosing children to play the parts of the various characters. Emphasise the fact that Jesus told Jairus to trust him. Write the word 'trust' in the middle of the large sheet of paper and display it so that all the group can see it easily. Ask the children whom they would trust to help them if they were ill. Draw arrows outwards from the word 'trust' and write the name of a person suggested by the children beside each arrow (mum, dad, doctor, nurse).

Ask the children to name other people they would trust to help them, both among their family and friends and in the wider community – such as helpers at playgroup, at school and in the local area (police, shopkeepers, traffic wardens, lollipop people). Record these on the sheet of paper. Invite the children to draw and colour in pictures of each person and to stick these next to the matching words (or names) on the sheet. Display the finished sheet on the wall.

Discussion

Explain that the story is taken from the Bible, which is the most important book in the Christian religion. Talk about the way in which lots of people trusted Jesus to help them when they were ill or in trouble. As the children suggest examples of people whom they trust, ask them to give their reasons for trusting these people. Emphasise the fact that these people are usually people we know well, or people whose job it is to help others.

Follow-up activities

✧ Discuss 'stranger danger'. Help the children to define what a stranger is, and what they should do if approached by one (walk or run away without saying a word). Use puppets to role-play 'stranger danger' situations (being offered sweets by a stranger in the park, being enticed into a car) and ask the children to tell the 'child' puppet what to do.

✧ Read the poem 'Sniff and tickle' in the Resources section on page 77.

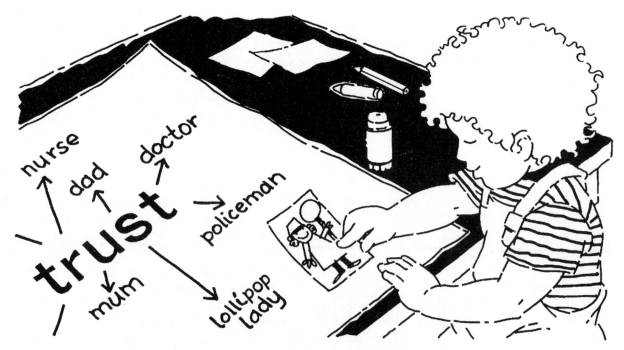

CHAPTER 7
DISPLAYS

Stimulus displays can play a vital part in introducing many aspects of the Myself project. They provide an interesting starting-point for discussion and can serve as a springboard for investigating other strands in the theme.

Whenever possible, involve the children in setting up the displays. They can help to make component parts and select appropriate backing paper, fabrics, objects and so on. Allow them to experiment with different arrangements and discuss how effective each is.

Always try to make the displays interactive. The children will gain much more from a display if they can contribute their own labels or objects which they are then encouraged to handle and touch freely. Similarly, if a display is the focus for a game or activity, the children are more likely to enjoy and remember the information it conveys.

The following pages suggest some ideas for display based on the Myself theme. Each activity relates to one of the main activity chapters earlier in the book.

BODY PARTS

What you need

A display board at child height, a large piece of thin coloured card, white paper, paints, paintbrushes, scissors, PVA adhesive, paper-clips, small pieces of white card for labels, a Stanley knife, felt-tipped pens.

What to do

Invite a child to paint a large simple picture of a child on the white paper. Encourage them to include as many different body parts as possible. When the painting is dry, cut it out and stick it on to the large piece of card.

On the small pieces of white card, write labels for the body parts on the painting. Arrange the labels on the card around the picture so that they are near to the corresponding body parts. Cut a slit above each label with the Stanley knife and use a paper-clip to hold the label in position.

Discussion

Carry out activities to familiarise the children with the picture and words. Ask a child to point to the label for a specific body part. Then suggest the children take turns to choose someone to find a particular label. Alternatively, point to a label and ask a child to read it. Then allow the children to choose labels for others to read.

Use the detachable labels for matching games. Remove some, or all, of

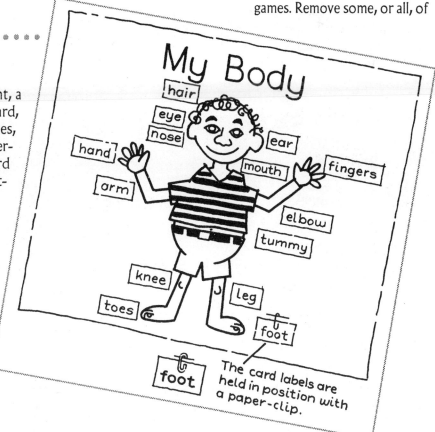

My Body

hair, eye, nose, ear, hand, mouth, fingers, arm, elbow, tummy, knee, leg, toes, foot, foot

The card labels are held in position with a paper-clip.

the labels and place them face down on a table. Ask individuals to choose a label and match it to the correct body part.

Encourage observation skills by turning some of the labels on the display upside down, removing some or swapping some round. Can the children say what is wrong with the picture and arrange the labels correctly?

Use this display in conjunction with the 'Heads, shoulders, knees and toes' activity described on page 11. Individuals can use a giant cardboard hand to point to the relevant parts of the body as the song is sung.

labels on shoe shapes   dark blue backing paper

Shoe prints

Match the shoes to the prints

print taken from sole of each shoe

collection of shoes

dark blue footprints on pale blue sugar paper for border

cardboard boxes draped in blue fabric

SHOE PRINTS

What you need

A display board covered in dark blue backing paper, strips of pale blue sugar paper for the border, blue paint, a shallow tray, white paper, two cardboard boxes (one large and one small), blue fabric, a collection of shoes (only one shoe from each pair), scissors, a stapler, felt-tipped pens.

What to do

Invite one or two children to help make the border by printing blue footprints with the paint on to the strips of pale blue sugar paper. To obtain good prints, make sure that the children's feet are evenly covered with paint and that they place their feet flat on to the paper. When dry, staple the border strips around the edge of the display board.

On the white paper, draw round a shoe twice, then cut out these outlines and use them as labels for the display. Write 'Shoe prints' on the labels and staple them in place near the top of the display.

Use the blue paint to take a print from the sole of each of the shoes on the white paper. When dry, cut out the shoe print and staple it to the display board. Write a label 'Match the shoes to the prints' and staple it in place at the bottom of the display.

Place the cardboard boxes together on one side of the display board. Drape the boxes with the blue fabric and arrange the shoes on the boxes so that the children have easy access both to the shoes and to the prints.

Discussion

Invite the children to look carefully at the sole of each shoe and to find the corresponding print on the display board. Encourage them to consider the size, shape and pattern on each sole.

Also use the display to stimulate discussion about footwear. Why do we wear shoes? Examine each shoe in detail. Who would wear it and when? Describe the size, shape, colour and materials used. What type of fastening does it have? Why do some shoes have a deep tread on the sole, while others have none?

Link this display to the 'Shoe mimes' activity on page 23.

ACTION WORDS

What you need

A display board covered in black backing paper, white paper, scissors, felt-tipped pens, Blu-Tack, a stapler, drawing pins, a camera.

What to do

Take photographs of the children involved in various activities. For example, they may be playing with sand or water or in the role-play area, building with construction toys, drawing, painting, reading or doing some physical activity on a climbing frame or in a play tunnel. Fix the photographs to the display board with the Blu-Tack. Write the question 'What can you do?' on to a card label and staple it in place at the top of the display board.

Make some concertina people using the white paper. Fold it as for a zigzag book, draw a large simple outline of a child on the front section and cut it out, leaving the hands attached at the paper's edge to act as a hinge. Repeat this so you have several strings of people. Use a drawing pin to fix each concertina of people (folded up) on to the display board amongst the photographs.

word by writing it on to one of the concertina people. For example, the children may suggest jumping, sliding, painting, splashing and building. Unfold one of the concertina people for each new word. Have some extra blank concertina people available, so that the children can continue to add new action words over the next few days. Encourage them to count the number of words they have thought of. What do they notice about the end of each word?

What can you do?

running · sliding · jumping · painting

Concertina people made from paper to use as labels for 'action' words

black backing paper

photographs of children involved in activities.

Discussion

Allow the children a period of time to study the photographs individually and then gather them around the display. Talk about the photographs, identifying the children in them and the activities they are doing.

Explain that you want the children to think of as many 'action' words as possible to describe the activities in the photographs. Record each action

HAIR CARE

What you need

A simple version of the story of Rapunzel (as can be found in *Fairy Tales*, retold by Brian Morse, Ladybird), a tall narrow cardboard box, scissors, paint, household paintbrushes, black sugar paper, PVA adhesive, glue sticks, white paper, felt-tipped pens, long strips of yellow paper, a small table draped in yellow fabric, hair care items such as shampoo, conditioner, combs, brushes, a towel, scissors, rollers and a hair dryer, decorative accessories such as slides, combs, ribbons, bands, bows and beads, a wig on a stand.

Preparation

Read the story of Rapunzel to make sure that the children will recognise her in the display.

What to do

Choose two or three children to help make Rapunzel's tower. Open one end of the cardboard box, remove the flaps and cut crenellations into the top edges of the box (an adult will need to do this). Paint the box to look like a tower and leave to dry.

Cut large, arched window shapes from black sugar paper and stick one window at the top of the front of the tower. Ask a child to draw and colour Rapunzel's face, then cut it out and stick it on to the window.

Use the long yellow strips of paper to make a long plait for Rapunzel. Add a speech bubble saying 'How should I look after my hair?' Attach the remaining windows to the other walls of the tower; but only stick down the top half of each window, leaving the bottom half to be lifted like a flap. Under each window flap, write a label to answer Rapunzel's question. For example, the labels could say 'Wash it', 'Dry it', 'Cut it', 'Watch out for head lice', 'Decorate it', and so on. Add a

large label under the picture of Rapunzel saying 'Rapunzel's tower'.

Place the table covered with yellow fabric near to the tower, and display the various hair care items on it. Place the wig on the stand close to the decorative items. Add a 'Hair care' label to the display.

Discussion

Allow the children time to look freely at the display. Gather them around the display and make sure that they recognise the Rapunzel character and can read her speech bubble. Focus attention on each window label in turn. Ask a child to lift the flap and read the label, then ask the children to identify the items in the display which relate to that label. Talk about each item in turn and discuss the importance of hair care. Invite the children to make new windows with different labels and bring hair care items of their own to add to the display.

During free play, allow the children to take turns to put the decorative items on to the wig. Use the display to inspire a project that involves setting up a 'hairdresser's'. As well as all the hair care items listed above, include mirrors (safety glass), magazines, cups of coffee, signs and posters showing different hairstyles. Remember to make sure children do not share combs or brushes. Use the opportunity to discuss head lice and how to prevent them.

CHAPTER 8
ASSEMBLIES

Assemblies, by their very nature, bring people together, and in demonstrating the many aspects of our lives that we all have in common can help to foster collective awareness and a sense of belonging.

AN ASSEMBLY ON FAMILIES

A child's family is the lynchpin of his or her life, and as such, any work on the subject must be completely free of value judgements. It is important that the children understand this and are not misled into discrimination of any kind.

This chapter suggests ideas for assemblies on the theme of 'Myself' and includes activities, prayers and songs.

Before holding the assembly, do some work to establish that families and family life are often different but that all are equally important. Ask the children to draw pictures or write stories and poems about their own families and then present them to each other.

Introduction

Introduce the assembly by telling an anecdote from your own family life. Recount, perhaps, some moment when you became totally exasperated with your family – but once you cooled down, you realised you wouldn't want to be without them.

What to do

Tell the children they are going to act out a little play that will demonstrate relationships, as well as how each nuclear or extended family is part of the complicated web of the greater family (humanity) to which we all belong.

Ask two or three children to come forward and sit in a row at the front. These are the children of the family. Discuss the words 'brother' and 'sister'.

Ask two more children to come forward to be the parents of the children. These are the 'mother' and 'father'.

Three more children can come forward to be 'sisters' and 'brothers' of the 'mother' and 'father'. These are the 'aunts' and 'uncles'.

Select more children to come forward to be the children of the 'aunts' and 'uncles'. These now become 'nieces' and 'nephews', as well as 'cousins'.

Four more children can come forward to act as the 'parents' of the first set of 'parents' and the 'grandparents' of the first set of children, who are now also 'grandchildren'. Further children can represent other relations – for example, the partners of aunts and uncles, and the parents or siblings of these partners. Allow more children to

come forward and make up more sets of aunts, uncles, cousins and so on – until you've used up as many children as possible from your group.

If there are many one-parent or step-parent family children in your group, include step-parents and their children, as well as the extra grandparents.

Many children also have godparents and sometimes don't understand how these 'fit' into the complicated web of relationships, so include godparents (and adults who fulfill a parallel role in other religious traditions) as well.

The confusion as the children try to remember how they are related to each other can add to the amusement of the play.

Reflection

Lead the children to consider their family lives: how they don't always see eye-to-eye with everyone, but how forgiveness and love can go a long way towards healing any hurts or rifts that can occur. With so many people in a family, all of whom are different, it wouldn't be fair to expect everybody to get on with everybody else – but the more people there are in a family, the more scope there is for love and the warmth of security.

Prayer

Dear God, We thank you for all our own families and for all the people we love and care for. We pray for you to look after them. We pray also for you to love and care for all those people who haven't got a family or a loving home. Please let them know that somebody cares about them. Amen.

Close the assembly with the song 'The Family of Man' from *The Complete Come and Praise Songbook* (BBC Books).

AN ASSEMBLY ON THINGS WE CAN DO

Before the assembly, spend time discussing the different things that the children can 'do'. Consider different areas of their life: for example, *physically* they may be able to jump up and down on two feet; *mentally* they may be able to recognise numbers and letters; *socially* they may be able to show caring and kindness to others.

Ask them to bring in photographs of themselves as babies, if possible. If they cannot get photographs, they could draw or cut out a picture of what they think they might have been like. Let them stick their picture or photo on to a piece of card, leaving space below or around the picture to add writing.

Tell each child to choose one thing that they are able to do now which they couldn't do when they were a baby. Try to achieve a good balance of physical activities, mental activities, social and language skills, so that no children feel that their skills aren't as advanced as those of their peers. It may be helpful to make the point that this assembly is a *sharing* time, not a *showing off* time. Help them to write a poem or a story about the thing they are able to do which they can copy on to the piece of card with their picture. If their writing skills are limited they could draw or paint instead. Help them to find the right words.

Introduction

Introduce the assembly by talking about something that you can do: some skill that you have developed even though when you were little you thought you would never be able to do it. Tell the children how you worked and practised to sharpen your skill, even though sometimes you felt like giving up, and how proud you are of your achievement now.

What to do

Ask some of the children to show their pictures to the others and act out their achievements. As one child shows what he can do, select another child to describe the achievement. This will involve more children in the presentation, and will also give children who feel they have very limited achievements a chance to show, and polish, their language skills. Make sure that all the children realise that different people can do different things: there is no hierarchy of achievements. It would be helpful if an adult colleague would be willing to show how she can't do something you can do, but that she is able to do something different. A small, light-hearted demonstration should give the children added insight.

Reflection

Help the children to realise that just because they are finding something hard to do at the moment, that doesn't necessarily mean they will never be able to do it. Encourage them to think of ways in which they can help themselves to develop skills, and try to motivate them towards positive attitudes and good self-esteem.

Prayer

Dear God, Thank you for all the things that we can do. Help us to know that what we can do is what makes us ourselves, different from everyone else. Help us to remember that we should never say 'I can't' because it stops us trying. We must try, try, try again until we can do it. Thank you for giving us the chance to learn to do things. Help us always to do those things which are kind to the world. Amen.

End the assembly with a 'Simon says' game, keeping the activities very simple and quiet. Lead the children, through 'Simon says', into leaving the assembly like little mice.

Include the song 'I can climb' from *Every Colour Under the Sun* (Ward Lock Educational).

AN ASSEMBLY ON BIRTHDAYS

Every child can feel involved in an assembly on the theme of birthdays.

Before the assembly, make sure that the children who are performing know when their birthday is. Explain that we all have a birthday every year and that birthdays tell us how old we are. Most of the children will probably know their age next birthday, but not the date of the birthday. Do some work on the months of the year to help familiarise the children with the names and the sequence of the months. Make a large coloured label for each month, and give one or two children responsibility for holding the label during the assembly.

Sort the children into groups according to their birthday months before they go into the assembly. Find out, before the assembly, if any child present will have a birthday on that day, or during that particular week.

Introduction

Introduce the birthday theme. Ask the children to guess what your assembly is going to be about from the clues you provide, such as: *Some people have had more than others. Old people have had lots, but small children haven't had many at all. You can count them but you can't keep them. When you have one of your own, you can't give it away to anybody else.* If the children need easier clues, try: *When somebody has theirs, you give good wishes or cards and presents to them. Sometimes we have parties on them. Often we have a cake with candles to blow out.*

What to do

Ask the children with the month name labels to hold them up in the correct order, and the children in the audience can hold up their hands when their birthday month is shown. The rest of the children could recite the month names with you while this is going on.

Most children will think about the cards and presents they receive for their birthday, but it is a good teaching point for them to focus upon the idea of *giving* and celebrating someone else's birthday. After mentioning their own presents (you can't really miss this out altogether!), ask the children to show pictures they have drawn or painted of another member of their family when it's their birthday. They could read out, or tell, stories about what they give to friends and family on their birthdays and how these presents are received.

The children will be interested in the fact that not all countries and cultures observe birthdays as we do. In some countries 'name' days are celebrated, and children get cards and presents on their own Saint's day rather than on their birthday. In other countries, age is relatively unimportant and birthdays are not honoured at all. Thai children *give* gifts to the Temple as thanks to the mother who gave them birth.

Reflection

Encourage the children to think about the fact that birthday gifts do not have to be *bought,* expensive or otherwise. The nicest gifts they can give someone are often those that are free: a smile, a friendly word, a hug, an invitation to join in a game.

Prayer

Thank you, Lord, for special days. Thank you for all the cards and gifts and special happiness other people give to us on our birthdays. Please help us to remember that giving and making other people happy is a good way of making ourselves happy. Amen.

If any child has a birthday in the week of the assembly, the children can all stand up and sing 'The Birthday Song' together.

Let the children leave the assembly thinking about the kinds of things they could do for others as special birthday gifts.

'The Birthday Song' can be found in *Tinder Box* (A&C Black).

Collective Worship in Schools

The assemblies outlined here are suitable for use with children in nurseries and play groups, but would need to be adapted for use with pupils registered in schools. As a result of legislation enacted in 1944, 1988 and 1993, there are now specific points to be observed when developing a programme of Collective Acts of Worship in a school.

Further guidance will be available from your local SACRE — Standing Advisory Council for RE.

SONGS

I'M ALIVE SHANTY

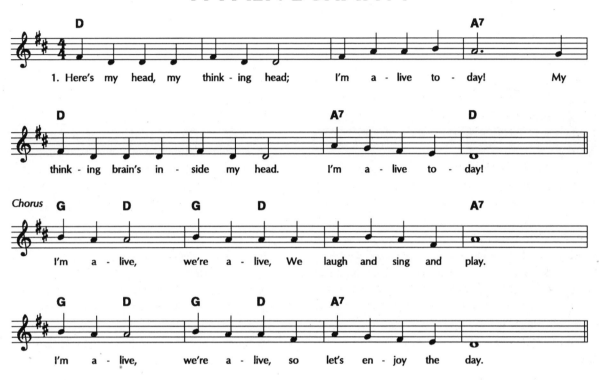

1. Here's my head, my thinking head; I'm a - live to - day! My think - ing brain's in - side my head. I'm a - live to - day!

Chorus

I'm a - live, we're a - live, We laugh and sing and play.

I'm a - live, we're a - live, so let's en - joy the day.

2. Here's my eyes, my seeing eyes;
I'm alive today!
I see the world through my eyes.
I'm alive today!

Chorus

3. Here's my mouth, my speaking mouth;
I'm alive today!
I talk and sing with my mouth.
I'm alive today!

Chorus

4. Here's my nose, my smelling nose;
I'm alive today!
I smell the world with my nose.
I'm alive today!

Chorus

5. Here am I, all of me;
I'm alive today!
And that's the way I want to be.
I'm alive today!

Chorus

Ian Henderson-Begg

THE BIRTHDAY SONG

Rhythmic

Go - ing to a par - ty, Sit - ting in a cir - cle, will it be me or you?

If you've got a birth - day In the month of *Au - gust This is what you've got to do.

> *Invent an action or forfeit for children with birthdays in August or whichever month you have chosen. Use this song to teach the order of the months, or pick a month at random for fun. During the first two lines the children should be seated in a circle. They should alternate two leg pats with two hand claps.

Ann Bryant

THAT HAT!

When I put this hat on, I'll be some - one else. Can you guess who

Child chooses a hat and puts it on.

I am When I'm not my - self?

Now you are a *sai - lor With a sai - lor's hat, When I am a

Child does actions for a sailor, for example, climb the rigging, coil the rope and so on.

sail - or, I do this and that.

This will change according to the type of hat.

Peter Morrell

WHAT'S THAT FACE?

What's that grum - py face in the mir - ror? Tell me now who can it be?

What's that grum - py face in the mir - ror? Does it look a bit like me?

Close my eyes, count to three, *(clap clap clap)* o - pen them and what do I see?

Other verses can be added, pulling appropriate faces.

What's that happy face in the mirror?
What's that ugly face in the mirror?
What's that cheeky face in the mirror?
What's that angry face in the mirror?

Debbie Campbell

IT'S HARD TO SAY YOU'RE SORRY

Some-times it's hard to say you're sor-ry._____ Some-times it's
hard to say you're wrong._____ When you're hurt-ing in-side you must
swal-low your pride and try to be grown-up and strong._____
Some-times it's good to talk things o-ver._____ You'll feel much
bet-ter in the end._____ Some-times it's hard to say you're
sor-ry_____ but it's eas-i-er than los-ing your best friend.

Debbie Campbell

SHOE CHOOSE TUNE

With sole

1. If I could choose what shoes to have, some wel - ling - tons I'd wear.

Repeat this part adding in extra words each time.

Splish splosh here. Splish splosh there. Splish splosh splish splosh ev - 'ry - where. If

I could choose what shoes to have, wel - ling - tons they'd be.

2. If I could choose what shoes to have,
   Some dancing shoes I'd wear.
   Tip-tap here. Tip-tap there.
   Tip-tap, tip-tap everywhere.
   Splish splosh here. Splish splosh there.
   Splish splosh, splish splosh everywhere.
   If I could choose what shoes to have,
   Dancing shoes they'd be.

3. If I could choose what shoes to have,
   Some flip-flop shoes I'd wear.
   Flip-flop here. Flip-flop there. etc.

4. If I could choose what shoes to have,
   Some horse's shoes I'd wear.
   Clip-clop here. Clip-clop there. etc.

5. If I could choose what shoes to have,
   Some slippers I would wear.
   Creep, creep here. Creep, creep there. etc.

Clive and Thomas Barnwell

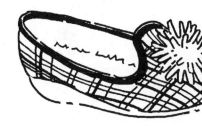

I USE MY HANDS

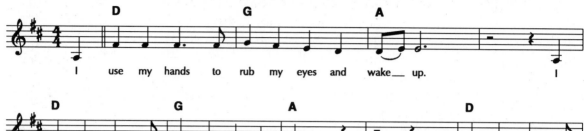

I use my hands to rub my eyes and wake up. I

use my hands to help me out of bed. I use my hands to

dress and do my clothes up. *(clap clap)* I use my hands to wash my

face *(clap clap)* and comb my hair *(clap clap)* a-cross my head. Thumb, fin-gers,

knuck-les and nails, palms and wrist to let you give your hand a twist.

2. I use my hands to hold a knife and fork in
I use my hands to hold my cup of drink
I use my hands to help me when I'm talking
I use my hands   *clap clap*
to hold high   *clap clap*
and tell teacher   *clap clap*
what I think.   *clap clap*
Thumbs, fingers, knuckles and nails, etc.

3. I use my hands to rock our baby's pram with
I use my hands to touch his face and hair
I use my hands to spread his bread and jam with
I use my hands   *clap clap*
to feed him while   *clap clap*
he's sitting in   *clap clap*
his high chair.   *clap clap*
As for verse 2.

4. I use my hands to play or read a book with
I use my hands to clap or bang a drum
I use my hands to weigh things and to cook with
I use my hands   *clap clap*
for writing words   *clap clap*
for painting pictures   *clap clap*
for having fun.   *clap clap*
                    As for verse 2.

David Moses

THE TOOTH SONG

The teeth pop up and the teeth pop down and the teeth turn a-round all day. The den-tist's go-ing mad, 'cos the teeth are ve-ry bad, and the one on the end keeps run-ning a-way.

Form one long line, two shorter lines or four very short lines, depending on how many times you want to go through the song! The number of children in each line is the number of repetitions. For 'pop up' the children reach two hands up; for 'pop down' they bob down and touch the ground. At 'turn around all day' they turn around; at 'going mad' they fold their arms; at 'very bad' they wag their index fingers; and at 'running away' the child on one end of the line goes to the other end.

Ann Bryant

LOOK RIGHT, LOOK LEFT

Look right, look left, look right a-gain, When-e-ver you cross the road.___ Look

road.___ A car may be ap-proach-ing or a lor-ry with its load.___ Look

right, look left, look right a-gain, When-e-ver you cross the road.___

Clive Barnwell

MY SHADOW

1. When I'm go-ing out to play, On a ve-ry sun-ny day, There's

some-thing that won't go a-way, My sha-dow!

2. When I dance and turn around,
It does the same thing on the ground.
It cannot make a single sound –
That shadow!

3. Everything that I can do
That silly shadow does it too.
I'm sure there's one that follows you –
Your shadow!

Jean Gilbert

PHOTOCOPIABLE RESOURCES

ACTION RHYMES AND POEMS

TOMMY THUMB

Tommy Thumb, Tommy Thumb, where are
you?
Here I am, here I am,
How do you do?
Peter Pointer, Peter Pointer, where are you?
Here I am, here I am,
How do you do?
Middleman Tall, Middleman Tall, where are
you?
Here I am, here I am,
How do you do?
Ruby Ring, Ruby Ring, where are you?
Here I am, here I am,
How do you do?
Baby Small, Baby Small, where are you?
Here I am, here I am,
How do you do?

Actions
Children show and wiggle the relevant finger as it
appears.

HERE WE GO ROUND THE MULBERRY BUSH

Here we go round the mulberry bush,
The mulberry bush, the mulberry bush,
Here we go round the mulberry bush
On a cold and frosty morning.

e.g. This is the way we . . .
clap our hands
take big strides
jump along
tiptoe home
sink into bed
clean our teeth
eat our lunch
. . . and so on.

Actions
This is an action rhyme which can introduce body
actions and everyday activities, as you choose. The
children skip in a ring for the first four lines, then
stop and perform whatever actions you wish to
introduce.
   You can also substitute a child's name for 'we',
allowing the child chosen to select an action for the
rest of the children to follow.

I CAN

I **can** count to ten,
Touch my toes,
Fasten buttons
And tie bows.

I **can** clean my teeth,
Wash my face,
Brush my hair
Into place.

I **can** stand up straight,
See how tall!
Or curl up tight
Round and small.

I **can** walk quickly
Or stand still,
Pretend to climb
Up the hill.

I **can** run and leap,
Skip and hop.
I can climb up
To the top.

I **can** taste and touch,
Hear and smell.
What a lot I
Can do well!

Tomorrow I'll try
Something new.
Change 'I can't' to
'I can do!'

Rozalia Makinson

Actions

Verse 1

Children touch each finger and thumb of both hands.

Bend over and touch toes with both hands, pointing fingers downwards. Pretend to fasten three buttons using right hand — at waist, chest and neck level.

Put hands at waist level, with the finger tips almost touching. Wriggle fingers three times, then move both hands sideways until the forearms are parallel.

Verse 2

Use the index finger as an imaginary toothbrush and mime cleaning teeth. With each hand open, make circular movements near (but not touching) each cheek for face-washing. With a clenched fist, make movements from the top of the head to shoulder level to brush hair.

Verse 3

Stand still and straight with arms down the sides.

Stand on tip-toe and stretch arms up. Sit down and slowly tuck in head, arms and legs to make a ball.

Verse 4

Mime walking quickly (on the spot). Stop all movements and stand still with arms at the sides like statues. Crouch down and slowly rise, swinging arms backwards and forwards until standing. Keep swinging arms as though climbing.

Verse 5

Run on the spot, leap forwards then back, skip forwards and back and hop, then stand still to regain balance. Pretend to climb again, as in Verse 4; but when at the top, put hand at eyebrow level as if looking into the distance.

Verse 6

The children can pretend to drink from a cup, then touch the palm of the left hand with the fingertips of the right hand.

Cup hand to ear then crook index finger and touch under the nose, and imagine your favourite smell.

Count off the things using the fingers, as in Verse 1.

Verse 7 (optional)

Look as if you're thinking of something new to do.

Frown for 'I can't', then smile and be happy for 'I can do!'

SNIFF AND TICKLE

I hate it when my nose is sniffy.
Sniff, sniff, sniff,
WHEEZE!

I like it when it starts to tickle.
Tickle, tickle, tickle,
SNEEZE!

Judith Nicholls

INSIDE

There are lots of things
They won't let me do –
I'm not big enough yet
They say.
So I quietly wait
Till I'm all grown up
And I'll show them all,
One day.
I could show them now
If they gave me the chance.
There are things I could do
If I tried.
But nobody knows,
No nobody knows, that I'm
Really a giant
Inside.

Irene Yates

THE END

When I was One
I had just begun.

When I was Two
I was nearly new.

When I was Three
I was hardly Me.

When I was Four
I was not much more.

When I was Five
I was just alive.

But now that I'm Six
I'm as clever as clever
So I think I'll stay Six now
For ever and ever.

A. A. Milne

HOW DO I FEEL?

How do I feel?
My face can't lie —

with furrowed brow
and narrowed eye

and zipped up teeth
that want to bite,

you'll know I'm looking
for a fight.

How do I feel?
My face can't lie —

it's like the sun
up in the sky,

with eyes like worms
bridged up to kiss.

I'm happy when
I look like this.

Gina Douthwaite

I LIKE TO HEAR

I like to hear the telephone ringing.
I don't like to hear my sister singing.

I like to hear sausages sizzling.
I don't like to hear the baby grizzling.

I like to hear dinosaurs roaring.
I don't like to hear my dad snoring.

John Foster

WALKING ROUND
THE ZOO

Walking round the zoo,
What did I see?

A prowling tiger
That growled at me.

Walking round the zoo,
What did I see?

A parrot that squawked
And winked at me.

Walking round the zoo,
What did I see?

A bucketful of fish
For the penguin's tea.

Walking round the zoo,
What did I see?

A monkey that pointed
And laughed at me!

John Foster

QUIET AS MICE

Quick —
be quiet as mice.
Don't make a sound.
Shhhh.

Quick — sit.

Upon the ground
without a sound!

Quick — stand.

Hold out your hand
without a sound.

Quick — hop.

To the baker's shop
without a sound.

Quick — skip.

Don't slippety slip
without a sound.

Pie Corbett

THE I-DON'T-WANT-TO-GO-TO-BED DANCE!

First, look busy!

Busy on the landing,
busy with your bricks;
busy in the kitchen,
a puzzle still to fix!

Busy with a storybook,
busy with TV;
busy watching **anything**,
'Five minutes left to see!'

Busy with your brother,
busy with the cat;
even busy washing up
or something good like that!

Busy at the table,
busy on the floor;
busy, busy, busy,
'Oh Mum, **5** minutes more

. . . **please**?'

But Mum
said
'BED!'

Judith Nicholls

ANIMAL SOUNDS WE CAN MAKE

After we count three
show us who
you can be —
one, two, three —

ROAR – like a lion prowling.

GRRRRR – like a tiger growling.

PURR – like a sleepy cat.

SQUEAK – like a flying bat.

BARK – like an angry dog.

CROAK – like a funny frog.

Pie Corbett

WHO?

Who will
never leave
always play
never hide
always stay
at my side
every day. . . ?

My
pretend
friend!

Judith Nicholls

SOMETIMES I PRETEND

Sometimes I pretend
I am a giant
With feet so HUGE
I squash the houses
In our street
Each time I move!

Sometimes I pretend
I am an ant,
With feet so small
I tiptoe by
And no one knows
I'm there at all!

Trevor Harvey

MY SHADOW

I stand in the sun
And my shadow
Stretches out flat from my feet.

I start to walk
And my shadow
Walks slowly off down the street.

I start to run
And my shadow
Runs away from me in the heat.

I sit down to rest
And my shadow
Sits down in front of the seat.

I cannot get rid of my shadow
No matter how hard I try,
Unless I stand in the shade
Or a cloud blots the sun from the sky.

John Foster

BEDTIME IN SUMMER

In summer, it's light
When I go to bed;
The sun's wide awake
As I bury my head
Between the sheets,
So crisp and white,
And try to sleep
Sweet dreams all night.

BUT

the puppy next door

Begins to yap
And a branch on my window
Goes 'tip tap tap'.

No wonder the sun
Is shining bright –
It's **TOO EARLY FOR BED**
On this fine summer's night!

Trevor Harvey

STORIES

THE NEW DUNGAREES

This is the story of a little girl called Daisy and her baby brother called Teddy. Now Daisy had just started school when this story happened, but Teddy was still at home with his mummy.

The story I want to tell you is about the time that Teddy had been invited to visit his friend James. Do you know James? He is Teddy's friend and lives just down the road.

Mummy dressed Teddy in a new pair of dungarees. They were blue and had red braces. Teddy looked very smart. His mummy said to him, 'Whatever happens, don't get your new clothes dirty. Do you understand?'

Teddy sucked his thumb and nodded his head. He did understand, but he didn't say anything.

They walked Teddy down the road till they came to James' house, and Teddy's mummy left him there while she went to the Post Office.

Teddy ran straight into James' bedroom. There was a new set of felt-tipped pens lying on the bed. Now when he is at home Teddy is not allowed to use felt-tipped pens. Can you guess why? Yes — sometimes he forgets to draw on the paper. He once drew a large monster on the back of Mum's sofa! And when he was very small he scribbled on the bathroom wall!

James' mummy gave the two boys a large pad of paper to draw on. Then she went into the kitchen to get their dinner ready. She was going to cook a Shepherd's Pie.

While she chopped the carrots she could hear lots of giggling. Oh good, she thought, James and Teddy are enjoying themselves. While she cut up the potatoes she could hear lots of laughing. Oh good, she thought. James and Teddy are enjoying themselves. While she was cutting up the onion she could hear the two boys talking in loud voices. Oh good, she thought. They are having such fun together. But while the Shepherd's Pie was cooking there was a silence. Oh dear, she thought. I wonder what they are doing now? James' mummy didn't like it when James was too quiet.

She crept down the corridor towards James' bedroom. There was not a sound coming from the room. She turned the doorknob as quietly as she could and peeped into the room. It was quite empty. Oh dear, she thought. I wonder where those two have got to.

Just then she heard a noise from the bathroom. It was the sound of running water. James' mummy stood outside the bathroom door and listened. She could hear Teddy saying, 'Pass the soap, James,' and she could hear James saying, 'Let's keep on trying.'

What good boys, thought James' mummy. They are washing their hands before dinner. She opened the door to help them. But they were not washing their hands.

James and Teddy were standing in the bath — and THEY HAD NO CLOTHES ON! And — they were COVERED in felt-

tipped marks, all over. They were covered in blues and reds and greens. Great splodges of colour, hundreds of dots like measles, and lines and squiggles all over their bodies. And Teddy had a huge funny face drawn on his back. James had drawn that.

They were busy trying to scrub the felt-tipped marks off.

Much later, when Teddy's mummy came to bring him home, she said, 'Oh you have done well, Teddy. Your dungarees are still quite clean. Why, they look brand new. I don't know how you managed that.' And Teddy said, 'I did some felt-tipped drawings but I was very careful, Mummy. I didn't get any on my clothes.'

And James' mummy said nothing.

Pie Corbett

SUMMER AT THE SWIMMING POOL

My name is Dinah and I am five years old. I live with my mother, father and older sister, Rachel, in Israel. I like the summer because then we can go swimming every morning.

In the summer it is so hot that we never use blankets on the beds, only sheets. Even then it is sometimes difficult to go to sleep at night. I like to keep the window and blinds open to make the room cooler. When my mother comes to wake me up in the morning, she'll say, 'Don't forget to shut the blinds, Dinah. You don't want to let all the heat into the house, do you?' In the summer we usually keep the blinds shut during the day so that the house stays nice and cool.

My parents let Rachel and me walk to the swimming pool on our own. It takes us about fifteen minutes. There are two swimming pools, a small, shallow one for children and a bigger one for adults. When my parents come swimming with us they let me go in the big pool with them, but when Rachel and I are on our own we have to use the small one. At one end of the small pool the water only comes up to my knees, but at the other end it is nearly over my head.

Usually we wear our swimming costumes underneath our shorts and T-shirts. When we get to the pool we just need to take them and our sandals off and we're ready to go in the water. We also take towels with us so we can lie on them if we get tired of swimming. Sometimes the pathway around the pool gets so hot that it hurts to stand on it. When this happens I splash some water on it to cool it down and shout for Rachel to bring my sandals.

The sun is so hot it never takes long for our swimming costumes to dry out. After a few minutes lying on our towels, we are dry enough to put on our clothes again and we can go home.

Lynn Lickiss

PHOTOCOPIABLE RESOURCES

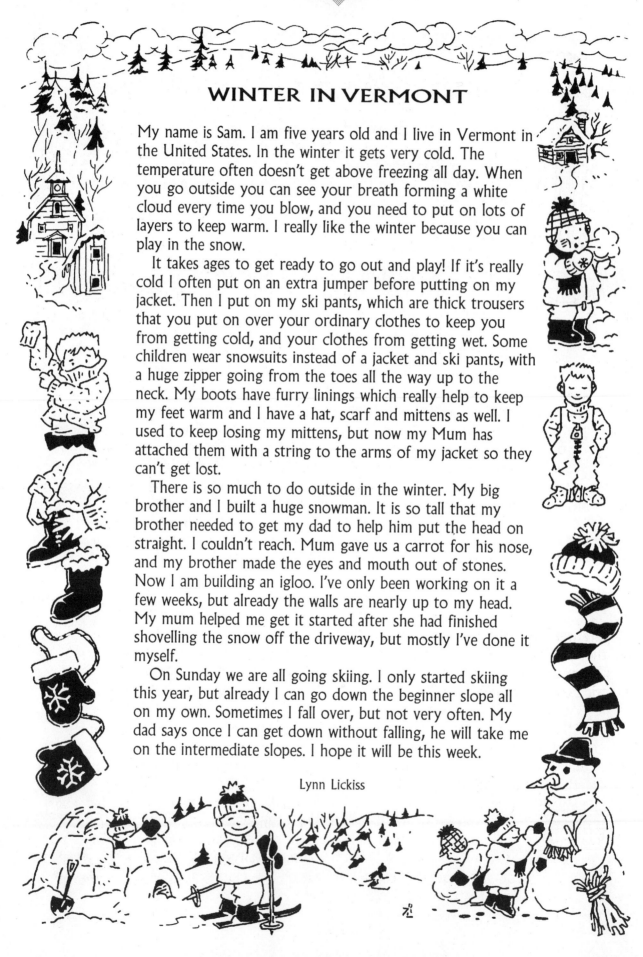

WINTER IN VERMONT

My name is Sam. I am five years old and I live in Vermont in the United States. In the winter it gets very cold. The temperature often doesn't get above freezing all day. When you go outside you can see your breath forming a white cloud every time you blow, and you need to put on lots of layers to keep warm. I really like the winter because you can play in the snow.

It takes ages to get ready to go out and play! If it's really cold I often put on an extra jumper before putting on my jacket. Then I put on my ski pants, which are thick trousers that you put on over your ordinary clothes to keep you from getting cold, and your clothes from getting wet. Some children wear snowsuits instead of a jacket and ski pants, with a huge zipper going from the toes all the way up to the neck. My boots have furry linings which really help to keep my feet warm and I have a hat, scarf and mittens as well. I used to keep losing my mittens, but now my Mum has attached them with a string to the arms of my jacket so they can't get lost.

There is so much to do outside in the winter. My big brother and I built a huge snowman. It is so tall that my brother needed to get my dad to help him put the head on straight. I couldn't reach. Mum gave us a carrot for his nose, and my brother made the eyes and mouth out of stones. Now I am building an igloo. I've only been working on it a few weeks, but already the walls are nearly up to my head. My mum helped me get it started after she had finished shovelling the snow off the driveway, but mostly I've done it myself.

On Sunday we are all going skiing. I only started skiing this year, but already I can go down the beginner slope all on my own. Sometimes I fall over, but not very often. My dad says once I can get down without falling, he will take me on the intermediate slopes. I hope it will be this week.

Lynn Lickiss

THE STORY OF JAIRUS' DAUGHTER

Jesus was in Galilee when a man named Jairus, who was a very important man in the synagogue, came to see him.

'I wish you would come and help me,' the man begged. 'My little girl is very, very ill. We are afraid that she's going to die. But if you come, and put your hands on her, she might get better again.'

Jesus told the man he would come to see the little girl. 'Don't be frightened,' he said. 'Just believe.'

The man, Jairus, trusted that Jesus would help him, so they set off for his house.

There were lots of people around Jesus, and they all began to follow. On the way, an old woman came from out of the crowd and tried to get near to Jesus. The old woman had been ill for a long time and although she had taken lots of different medicines, none of them had cured her. She'd heard about Jesus' miracles. She thought that if only she could touch him, her illness would go away.

The old woman touched Jesus' cloak.

Jesus turned around instantly. 'Who touched me?' he called.

The old woman was frightened, but she came forward and said that it was her. 'I was sick,' she said, 'but I knew if I could touch you I would be well again.'

Jesus smiled at her. 'Then go on your way,' he said. 'Because you believed in me, you are better now.'

While all this was happening, a messenger came from the house where Jairus lived. 'It's too late!' he said. 'There's no point in Jesus coming now – the little girl has died!'

But Jesus insisted.

When they got to the house, Jesus went into the little girl's bedroom to take a look at her. 'It's all right,' he said, 'she is only sleeping.'

Everybody laughed at him. 'She's not asleep,' they cried. 'She's dead!'

Jesus held the little girl's hand, very gently, and said, 'Get up.'

The girl opened her eyes and climbed down from the bed. Everybody was so surprised they couldn't believe what they were seeing.

But Jesus wasn't surprised at all. 'Give her something to eat,' he said. 'She's better now, and she's hungry.'

And then he went on his way, telling all the people not to let anyone know what they had seen.

Irene Yates

EVERYBODY'S DIFFERENT

Zoe and Samantha were twins.

They looked exactly the same as each other.

They sounded exactly the same as each other.

Everything they did, they did the same as each other.

'It's not fair,' said Zoe, 'when I look in the mirror I see Samantha instead of me.'

'It's not fair,' said Samantha, 'every time I look at Zoe I see myself instead of her.'

Mum said, 'That's not true. Zoe is Zoe. And Samantha is Samantha.'

'But I'm exactly the same as her!' said Samantha. 'I want to be different.'

'And I'm exactly the same as her!' wailed Zoe. 'I want to be different too!'

Mum tried her best.

When Zoe wore red clothes, Samantha wore green. And when Samantha wore blue clothes, Zoe wore yellow.

But it didn't really help.

'Because if people don't know who's wearing which colours then we still look the same!' the twins said. 'And if we still look the same, then we must be the same!'

'But you're not!' Mum said. 'You are two very different girls.'

'Well, I want to be myself,' said Samantha.

'And I want to be myself too,' said Zoe.

But still it wasn't easy.

If Zoe caught a cold, then Samantha caught a cold.

If Samantha got the measles, then Zoe got the measles.

'But that happens to all brothers and

sisters,' Mum said. 'It's because you live in the same house!'

'No!' cried Zoe and Samantha, 'It's because we're exactly the same.'

'Nonsense!' Mum said. 'No two people in the world are exactly the same. Everybody is different.'

'No!' cried the twins, 'We're exactly the same!'

'You're not,' said Mum, 'and I can prove it to you!'

Zoe and Samantha were puzzled. When they looked at each other, they looked exactly the same. How could Mum possibly prove they were different?

Without saying a word, Mum covered the kitchen table with newspaper. Then she got some big sheets of painting paper and some sticky red paint.

'What are you doing?' asked the girls.

'You'll see,' Mum said mysteriously. 'All we need now is a magnifying glass.'

'A magnifying glass?' said the girls, even more puzzled.

At last Mum was ready.

'In you come,' she called. 'Now — dip your thumbs into the paint.' She gave each twin a piece of painting paper. 'Now, press very carefully all over the sheet to make a thumb pattern.'

Zoe and Samantha giggled away as they made their thumb patterns, but they still couldn't understand what Mum was up to.

Mum picked up the magnifying glass.

'When you look through here,' she said, 'you can see things much bigger than they really are. And you're going to look at your thumbprints very, very carefully.'

Each girl peered through the magnifying glass at her own thumbprints. And then she looked at her sister's.

Through the magnifying glass they could see that each thumbprint had a little swirl of lines arranged very tightly in a pattern. And Zoe's pattern was very different from Samantha's.

'That's not all!' said Mum with a smile. 'Everybody in the whole wide world has their very own thumbprint — no matter how many people you meet, nobody will ever have a thumbprint exactly the same as yours! So you see — everyone is special, and not the same as anyone else at all!'

And Mum was right. Everyone is unique — including you! Why not try it for yourself and see?

Irene Yates

THEMES
for early years

Name _____

Jigsaw faces

◆ Draw lines to match the missing features to the puzzles.

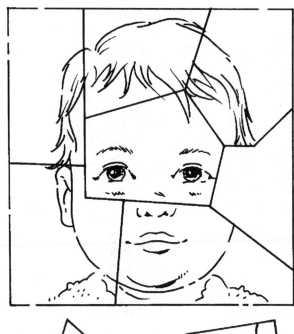

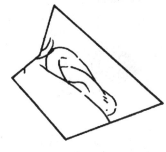

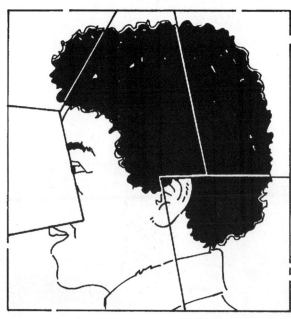

THEMES
for early years

Name _____

Match the hats

✦ Match the hats to the people.

fire-fighter

nurse

policewoman

lollipop person

THEMES
for early years

Name _____

Draw a route

◆ Draw a route home for the small doll and teddy.

THEMES
for early years

Name _____

Match the clothes

◆ Match the clothes to the dolls.

grandad   mummy   baby

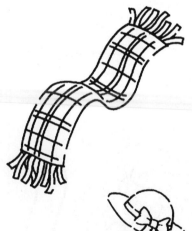

THEMES
for early years

Name _____

Bean bags

◆ Colour and count the bean bags.

THEMES
for early years

Clown faces

happy

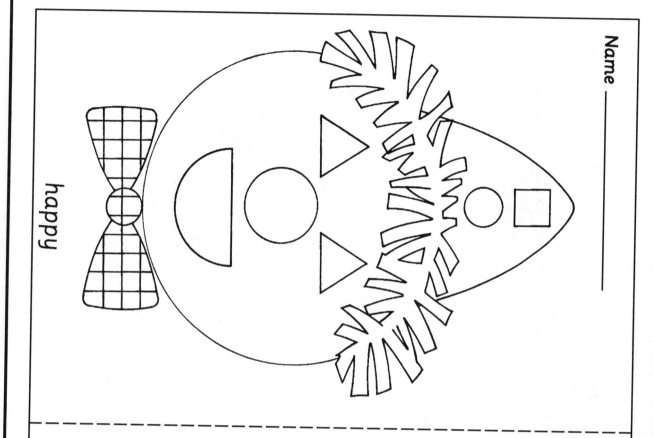

sad

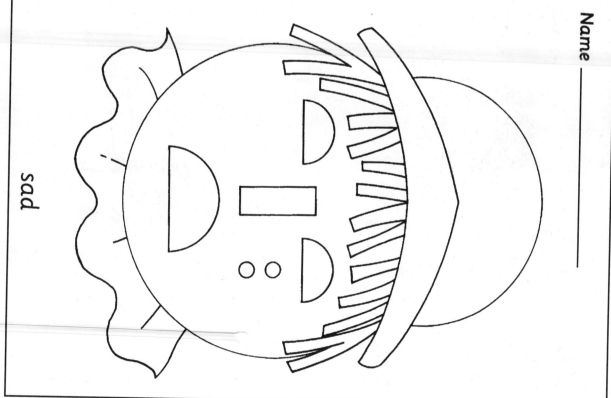

THEMES
for early years

Name _____

Draw a banana

✦ Draw a banana for each child.

✦ Draw an apple for each child.

✦ Draw a kiwi fruit for each child.

THEMES
for early years

Name _____

Recipe pictures

◆ Cut out the pictures and stick them in the right order.

RECOMMENDED MATERIALS

INFORMATION BOOKS
My Body B. Matthias and R. Thomson (Franklin Watts).
All About You C. and A. Anholt (Heinemann).
Body Bits R. Thomson (Franklin Watts).
I Have Two Homes Althea (Dinosaur).
The House Where Jack Lives M. Crompton (Bodley Head).
Look at Hair R. Thompson (Franklin Watts).
How Do People Dress? E. Urai (Macdonald).
Caspar's Feet D. Tourneur (Burke).
Littlebody Books series: *Teeth; Eat; Drink; Grow* (Macdonald).
Lunchboxes Althea (Dinosaur).
Taking Care with Strangers K. Petty (Franklin Watts).
Be Safe series: *On the Road* (Franklin Watts).

STORY BOOKS
You'll Soon Grow into Them, Titch P. Hutchins (Bodley Head).
Avocado Baby J. Burningham (Picture Lions).
Gran and Grandpa H. Oxenbury (Walker).
I Want my Potty T. Ross (Picture Lions).
I Like Me N. Carlson (Picture Puffin).
Alfie's Feet S. Hughes (Picture Lions).
My Naughty Little Sister D. Edwards (Methuen).
Nancy No-size M. Hoffman (Methuen).
That's My Baby A. Lindgren (Methuen).
The Hollywell Family M. Kornitzer (Bodley Head).
Janine and the New Baby I. Thomas (Methuen).
This Little Baby's First Tooth L. Breeze (Orchard Books).
Grandfather J. Baker (André Deutsch).
Something Special D. McPhail (Picture Puffin).
Are We Nearly There? L. Baum (Methuen).
Bet You Can't P. Dale (Walker).
Look, There's My Hat M. Roffey (Piccolo).
Red is Best K. Stinson (OUP).
Blood and Plasters L. Berg (Methuen).

POETRY
Meet the Family (Collection) S. Grindley (Orchard Books).
A Kiss on the Nose (Collection) T. Bradman (Heinemann).
'Anger' from the *Tinderbox Assembly Book* S. Barratt (A & C Black).

Smile Please (Collection) T. Bradman (Young Puffin).
'Red for Danger' and 'Choosing Shoes' in *Playtime Activity Book* S. Strange (BBC).

MUSIC
'How many People Live in Your House?', 'I've Got a Body' and 'The Angry Song' from the *Tinderbox Song Book* (A & C Black).
'She's the Best Mum in the World' from *Sing a Song of Celebration* (Holt Rinehart Winston).
'When I am happy', 'Caring for myself' and 'Clothes' from *Sing As You Grow* (Ward Lock Educational).
'If You're Happy and You Know It' from *Sing a Song: 1* (Nelson).
'How do you feel today?' from *Songs from Play School* (BBC).

ART
Self-portraits by many artists including Rembrandt, Rubens, van Gogh and Cézanne.
'Charles IV and his Family' Goya.
'The Painter's Family in the Garden' Paul Gauguin.
'The Bellelli Family' Edgar Dégas.
'The Marriage' Henri Rousseau.
'Weeping Woman', 'Bird and Child', 'Mother and Son' Pablo Picasso.
'The Scream' Edvard Munch.
'Birthday' Marc Chagall.

GAMES AND PUZZLES
My Body set of jigsaw puzzles from Ravensburger. (Available in toy shops.)
Talkabout Puzzles floor jigsaw puzzles (including *Playground, Swimming Pool, Building Site, Playgroup* and *Summer & Winter*) from Orchard Toys. (Available in toy shops.)
Times of the Day and *Children at Play* wooden puzzles from Step by Step (Lavenham Road, Beeches Trading Estate, Yate, Bristol BS17 5QX).

DRAMA / PLAY RESOURCES
Resources available from Step by Step include *Multicultural Dolls, Hats, Ethnic Costumes, Dressing-up Clothes, 'United Families of Our World' Dolls, Multiethnic Family Puppets, Little Tikes Family Sets* and *Duplo World People*.

PHOTOCOPIABLE RESOURCES